Wordstruck

A Workbook on Building a Better English Vocabulary

M. E. Taylor, Ph.D., Linguistics

and

A. P. McNeill, Professor Emeritus of English

Table of Contents

Introduction

Wordstruck is a vocabulary development workbook for high school students (grades 8-12), college students, and intermediate or advanced English-as-a-second-language learners. Our approach to vocabulary development is novel because of its emphasis on analyzable word structure, i.e., English morphology, and on word building through productive affixation and bound and unbound word forms.

Working through *Wordstruck* students will achieve these goals:

- develop a more sophisticated vocabulary
- gain a deeper understanding of morphology and grammar
- develop a technique to analyze new words they encounter in their reading and listening
- employ trustworthy dictionaries (e.g., Miriam Webster and the Oxford English Dictionary) more effectively
- improve their spelling
- raise their literacy level.

The first part of the workbook introduces analyzable words containing productive prefixes and suffixes; the second part continues working with affixes attached to bound and unbound word forms.

Each of the eleven units contains:

- a pretest and post-test
- a clear set of goals
- explanatory texts with examples and tables
- numerous exercises

The workbook also contains:

- a complete answer key
- a substantial glossary at the end of the book.

Because there is an emphasis on exercises with a complete answer key provided, the book is ideal for both self-study and classroom instruction.

Unlike other vocabulary development texts that concentrate on contexts and the vocabulary used in those contexts (e.g., restaurant, dental office, etc.), the outstanding feature of *Wordstruck* is the focus on morphology and word building based on sound linguistic principles. Although the contextual approach of other texts is valid, such an approach tends to ignore the complex morphology of English vocabulary. Though designed for students in high school and ESL learners, these linguistic principles will also help college students, whether in the arts or sciences, pre-med or pre-law.

In *Wordstruck* we have designed an easy-to-use textbook that will help students learn the essential linguistic principles needed to foster a more advanced vocabulary.

—Moira Taylor and Allan McNeill

UNIT 1

COMMON PREFIXES

Pretest: Test your knowledge about common English prefixes before doing this unit.

1. What does *ex-* mean in *ex-wife*?

2. What does *re-* mean in *refit*?

3. What are two major meanings of the prefix *sub-*?

4. Which is the prefix in *misbehave*? What does it mean?

5. What do *un-* and *dis-* have in common?

You will find the answers to these questions in the unit.

Definition: A **prefix** is something that is added to the beginning of a word and that changes the meaning of the word in a particular way.

English has many prefixes that are used to modify existing words. Some are in common use, while others are found in more technical vocabulary. In this unit you will learn some of the most common prefixes, those that will help you in speaking and reading everyday English.

Goals

- One goal of Unit 1 is to build longer words by adding prefixes to familiar words.
- Another goal is to understand unfamiliar words by analyzing them as familiar words with prefixes.

Some Common Prefixes

Familiar Word	Prefixed Word	Meaning
kind	unkind	'not kind'
do	redo	'do again'
cook	precook	'cook in advance'

The prefix *un-* in *unkind* means 'not' and adds this meaning to the base word *kind*. Similarly *re-* in *redo* adds the meaning of 'again' to the base word *do*, and *pre-* adds its meaning 'in advance' to *cook*. Once you know the form and the meaning of common prefixes like these, you will be able to start analyzing more unfamiliar words, and to remember their meanings more easily.

Examine the list of prefixes below and learn their meanings. Then attempt the exercises.

Table 1

Form	Meaning	Example
anti-	'opposed to, against'	antiwar 'opposed to war'
co-	'fellow'	co-pilot 'fellow pilot'
de-	'remove, remove from'	dethrone 'remove from the throne'
ex-	'former'	ex-actor 'former actor'
fore-	'before, beforehand'	foresee 'see beforehand'
mis-	'bad(ly), wrong(ly)'	misjudge 'judge badly'
pre-	'in advance'	precook 'cook in advance'
pro-	'favor, favoring'	pro-Canadian 'favoring Canada'
re-	'again'	recook 'cook again'
super-	'superior, exceeding'	superpower 'superior power'
un-	'not'	unkind 'not kind'

Some prefixes, like *ex-* and *co-*, are attached to the word with a hyphen. *Ex-wife* 'former wife', for example, has a hyphen, and so does *co-pilot* 'fellow pilot'. *Anti-* and *pro-* often occur with a hyphen, especially when the word to which they are attached refers to a nation: *pro-Canadian*, *anti-Canadian*. Most prefixes, however, do not occur with a hyphen.

Exercises: Table 1

1.1 Give the meaning of the following words by consulting the prefixes listed in the table.

Example: remake   'make again'

a.   prepay   _____

b.   misbehave   _____

c.   revisit   _____

d.   unfriendly   _____

e.   co-worker   _____

f.   ex-president   _____

g.   forewarn   _____

h.   antidemocratic   _____

i.   superwoman   _____

j.   defrost   _____

k.   pro-abortion   _____

1.2. Replace the underlined words by using the base word with a prefix from Table 1. Use the longer word in the same sentence.

Example: <u>Make</u> your bed <u>again</u>!

            <u>Remake your bed!</u>

a.   Jack is the <u>former husband</u> of my friend Mary.

    _____

b.   My neighbor is <u>opposed to unions</u>.

    _____

c.   It is <u>not wise</u> to spend all your money on clothes.

    _____

d.   A party <u>favoring logging</u> was elected.

    _____

e.   That child <u>understood</u> me <u>incorrectly.</u>

    _____

f.   The campers <u>cut</u> the wood <u>in advance</u> for their fire.

    _____

g.   Workers <u>removed ice from</u> the airplane's wings.

    _____

h.   Susan and Brian are the <u>fellow editors</u> of this newspaper.

    _____

i.   Mary claims that she can <u>tell beforehand</u> the future of her friends and
    relatives.

    _____

j.   The government has built a <u>superior highway</u> on Vancouver Island.

_____

Negative Prefixes

Several English prefixes express the meaning 'not'. They are called negative prefixes because they negate the base word. Examples are *unwise* 'not wise' and *nonathlete* 'not an athlete'. Another negative prefix is *dis-* 'not', as in *disagreeable* 'not agreeable'.

These prefixes are called *synonymous* because they have the same meaning. Some base words take *un-*, others take *non-* and still others take *dis-*. A few English words may take *un-* and *non-*, as in *unathletic* 'not athletic' and *nonathletic* 'not athletic'. If you are not sure whether a word exists or not, check it in a good dictionary. For example, *disagreeable* is listed as a word in the dictionary, but neither *nonagreeable* nor *unagreeable* is listed.

Table 2

Form	Meaning	Example
dis-	'not'	disagreeable 'not agreeable'
non-	'not'	nonathletic 'not athletic'
un-	'not'	unwise 'not wise'

Exercises: Tables 1 & 2

1.3 Replace the underlined words by using the base word with the prefix indicated in the parentheses. Use the longer word in the same sentence.
Example: Your bed is still <u>not made</u>! (*un-*)

            <u>Your bed is still unmade!</u>

a.   The man is <u>not honorable</u>. (*dis-*)

_____

Unit 1   12

b.   The girl who was <u>not happy</u> cried for an hour. (*un-*)

_____

c.   The boy is <u>not</u> a <u>smoker</u>. (*non-*)

_____

d.   Those comments were <u>not necessary</u>. (*un-*)

_____

e.   My mother was <u>not pleased</u> about my grades. (*dis-*)

_____

f.   Milk is <u>not acidic</u>. (*non-*)

_____

1.4 Break apart the following words by separating the prefix from the basic word, and give the meaning of each.

Example: unused   <u>un + used 'not used'</u>

a.   reused   _____

b.   mispronunciation   _____

c.   dislike   _____

d.   unsure   _____

e.   nonstick   _____

f.   desalt   _____

g.   nonreusable   _____

Prefixes with Multiple Meanings

A confusing fact about English prefixes is that many of them have more than one meaning. For example, *re-* means both 'again' and 'back'. So you have to remember the correct meaning of *re-* in a particular word. In *recook*, the prefix means 'again'; in *repay*, it means 'back', so *repay* means 'pay back'. You will be learning the most important meanings of the prefixes as we go through this section. Make sure you memorize the major meanings of each prefix.

Table 3

Form	Meanings	Example
co-	'together' 'fellow'	co-exist 'exist together' co-pilot 'fellow pilot'
dis-	'not' 'do the opposite of'	disapprove 'not approve' discontinue 'do the opposite of continue'
pre-	'in advance' 'before'	precook 'cook in advance' prehistory 'before (written) history'
re-	'again' 'back'	recook 'cook again' repay 'pay back'
semi-	'half' 'partly, partial'	semicircle 'half circle' semidarkness 'partial darkness' semi-civilized 'partly civilized'
sub-	'below, under' 'secondary'	subsoil 'below the soil' subcontract 'secondary contract'
un-	'not' 'do the opposite of'	unkind 'not kind' undress 'do the opposite of dress'

Exercises: Table 3

1.5 Create a word by adding a prefix to the base word.

Example: do the opposite of bend   <u>unbend</u>

a.   before dawn   _____

b.   turn back   _____

c.   manage together   _____

d.   below the conscious   _____

e.   partly cooked   _____

f.   do the opposite of fold   _____

g.   do the opposite of connect _____

1.6 Choose the correct meaning for the prefix in each word. Use the sentence as a clue to the right meaning.

Example:

You must <u>re</u>learn the prefixes in Table 1 if you have forgotten them.

      'again'

Ford Motors had to <u>re</u>call all the faulty cars in order to repair them.

      'back'

a.   The company's engineers chose May and September for their <u>semi</u>annual meetings.

      _____

b. This area of Australia is <u>semi</u>dry.

              _____

c. Don't <u>pre</u>judge Tom before you get to know him.

              _____

d. Jim and Helen had a <u>pre</u>-lunch drink in the restaurant.

              _____

e. <u>Sub-</u>zero temperatures are common in northern Canada.

              _____

f. The chief editor gave specific orders to her <u>sub</u>editors.

              _____

g. This meat is <u>un</u>cooked!

              _____

h. Please <u>un</u>wrap your birthday gift.

              _____

i. Wendy is a <u>co-</u>owner of this café; Dale is the other owner.

              _____

j. Paul Robinson and Jack Smith <u>co-</u>directed this movie.

              _____

k. The son's rude behavior to the guests <u>dis</u>honored his parents.

              _____

l.   Thieves are <u>dis</u>honest.

        _____

1.7 Using the word in the parenthesis, attach the correct prefix to create the appropriate word.

Example: below the moon (lunar)   <u>sublunar</u>

a.   under the sea (marine)   _____

b.   under the water (aquatic)   _____

c.   half yearly (annual)   _____

d.   partly able to read and write (literate)   _____

e.   partly dry (arid)   _____

f.   move again (locate)   _____

g.   shrink back (coil)   _____

h.   spring back (bound)   _____

i.   before marriage (marital)   _____

j.   before reading and writing (literate)   _____

1.8 Choose either the prefix *anti-* or *pro-*; then rearrange the sentence according to the model given.

Example:

        John dislikes opinions <u>opposed to the Americans</u>.

        John dislikes <u>anti-American</u> opinions.

a.　John dislikes feelings <u>hostile to the Canadians</u>.

　　John dislikes _____ feelings.

b.　John dislikes <u>policies which are hostile to the Cubans</u>.

　　John dislikes _____.

c.　Mary <u>favors the French</u>.

　　Mary is _____.

d.　Mary likes John's <u>views supporting the Japanese</u>.

　　Mary likes John's _____.

e.　Mary likes <u>companies which favor technology</u>.

　　Mary likes _____.

Post-test

Choose the appropriate prefix for each blank.

Example:　China is developing into a <u>super</u>power.

a.　Susan met her _____ boyfriend and his new girlfriend at the party.

b.　Fred drew a circle and then a _____ circle.

c.　You have to _____ do your homework because of all the mistakes.

d.　You have to _____ do your shoelaces before removing your shoes.

e.　_____ terranean creatures live below the ground.

f.   We've lost your application so you need to _____ apply for admission to the university.

g.   The baseball player _____ played the ball and the other team scored a run.

h.   The roast took four hours to _____ frost before it was ready to be cooked.

i.   Lions and elephants _____ exist on the plains of Africa.

j.   Dinosaurs _____ date humans.

k.   To _____ close information means to make it open to view.

UNIT 2

PREFIXES WITH SEVERAL FORMS

Pretest

1. What does *in-* mean in *incorrect*?

2. Is *im-* in *impolite* the same prefix as *in* in *incorrect*?

3. Why do several forms of the prefix *in-* exist?

4. What are the two major meanings for the prefix *en-* as in *ensure* and *emplace*?

You will find the answers to these questions in the unit.

Explanation: Some common prefixes have different forms depending on the word to which they are attached. For example, *in-* in *incorrect* 'not correct' changes to *il-* in *illiterate* 'not literate'. The form of the prefix depends on the first letter of the base word. Since *literate* begins with *l*, the prefix *in-* has the form *il-* in this case.

Goals

- A goal in Unit 2 is to recognize the various forms of the prefixes *in-* and *en-*.

- Another goal is learn the several meanings for *en-*.

Prefix *in-*

This prefix has the meaning 'not'. It negates the meaning of the base word to which it is attached.

Here are the different forms of the prefix *in-*. The form that appears depends on the letter at the start of the base word.

Table 1

Form	Example
in-	incorrect 'not correct' intolerant 'not tolerant' inaccurate 'not accurate'
il-	illiterate 'not literate'
ir-	irregular 'not regular'
im-	immature 'not mature' impossible 'not possible' imbalanced 'not balanced'

As you can see, the prefix *in-* changes to *il-* before *l*, and to *ir-* before *r*. It also changes to *im-* before *p* and *b* as well as before *m*. The prefix *in-* remains unchanged before letters other than *l, r, m, p, b*. Thus most words with this prefix will have the *in-* form.

Now you should be able to recognize the prefix *il-* in *illegal* and understand its meaning 'not', as well as the meaning of the whole word *illegal* 'not legal'.

Synonymous Prefixes

In Unit 1 you were introduced to the negative prefixes *un-*, *non-*, and *dis-*. You may now add *in-* to this group. They are all synonymous because they have the same meaning 'not'; however, they are not interchangeable. Compare *unlawful* to *illegal*, for example. Although the prefixes mean the same thing, you cannot prefix *un-* to *legal* or *il-* to *lawful*. If you are unsure about which prefix to use with a particular word, consult a good dictionary.

Prefix *en-*

This prefix has two major meanings. In many words it means 'to put into or onto', as in *enthrone* 'to put on a throne'. In many other words it means 'to make, to cause to be', as in *enslave* 'to make a slave, to cause to be a slave'. This prefix has only two different forms, shown in Table 2.

Table 2

Form	Example
en-	enslave 'to cause to be a slave' enthrone 'to put onto the throne'
em-	embitter 'to make bitter' emplace 'to put into position'

It is very predictable where you will find the different forms of *en-*: *em-* before *p* and *b* and *en-* before all other letters. *En-* is, therefore, the most common form of the prefix, but you need to recognize its other form, and to learn the two major meanings of this common prefix.

Exercises: Tables 1 & 2

2.1 Make the following sentences negative by attaching the appropriate form of the prefix *in-*.

Example: Your answer is <u>correct</u>.
           Your answer is <u>incorrect</u>.

a.   The water is <u>pure</u>.

     The water is _____ .

b.   His idea was <u>logical</u>.

     His idea was _____.

c.   She felt <u>secure</u> at school.

     She felt _____ at school.

d.   Mary behaved <u>rationally</u> when the professor failed her essay.

Mary behaved _____ when the professor failed her essay.

e.   His <u>ability</u> to do math is well known.

His _____ to do math is well known.

f.   There is a <u>balance</u> of trade between Canada and Mexico.

There is an _____ of trade between Canada and Mexico.

g.   Joanne behaved <u>responsibly</u> at work.

Joanne behaved _____ at work.

h.   Humans are <u>mortal</u>; gods are _____.

i.   She was invited to a <u>formal</u> dinner.

She was invited to an _____ dinner.

j.   The teacher said that Bill's handwriting was <u>legible</u>.

The teacher said that Bill's handwriting was _____.

2.2 Rewrite each sentence by replacing the prefix with *not*. You may have to restructure some of the sentences.

Examples: Your answer is <u>incorrect</u>.
            <u>Your answer is not correct</u>.

            She behaved <u>irresponsibly</u>.

Unit 2   23

She didn't behave responsibly

a.   Throwing paper airplanes is <u>improper</u> behavior during an exam.

_____

b.   They held the meeting at an <u>inconvenient</u> time.

_____

c.   At lunch Susan was <u>impolite</u> to my best friend.

_____

d.   Mary's reply was <u>irrelevant</u> to the teacher's question.

_____

e.   He behaved <u>insanely</u> at the dance.

_____

f.   James attended classes <u>irregularly</u>.

_____

2.3 Attach the appropriate form of the prefix *en-* to the underlined base word to create a word that corresponds to the meaning given.

Example: 'to put onto a <u>throne</u>'   <u>enthrone</u>

a.   'to put into <u>danger</u>'   _____

b.   'to cause to become a <u>body</u>'   _____

c.   'to put into a <u>rage</u>'   _____

d.   'to make <u>large</u>'   _____

e.   'to make <u>purple</u>'   _____

Unit 2   24

f.   'to give <u>force</u> to'   _____

g.   'to provide with <u>power</u>'   _____

h.   'to make <u>noble</u>'   _____

2.4 Replace the underlined word or words with the appropriate word from the list of words provided.

    ensure   embedded   emplaced   encircled
    enlivened   enrich   enlarged   entrust

Example: The rioters were <u>surrounded</u> by the riot police.

        <u>Encircled</u>

a.   The classroom was <u>made bigger</u> over the summer.

        _____

b.   The fossil was <u>covered</u> in the rock.

        _____

c.   His jokes <u>lit up</u> the party.

        _____

d.   Please <u>make certain</u> that the window is closed before you leave.

        _____

e.   The trip to London will <u>improve</u> my knowledge of English culture.

        _____

f.   The troops were <u>put into position</u> around the president's palace.

_____

g   While traveling, the parents <u>give the care of</u> their son to the grandparents.

_____

2.5 You know what Arctic and Antarctic refer to: Arctic refers to the north pole and Antarctic to the south pole.

a. What is the prefix in *Antarctic*?

b. What is the other form of the prefix and what does it mean?

c. What does the prefix specifically mean in *Antarctic*?

d. Why does the prefix take the form it does in *Antarctic*?

Post-test

Part A Attach the correct form of the prefix *in-* to the base word to make a word that corresponds to the given meaning.

Example: 'not polite'   <u>impolite</u>

a.   'not reparable'   _____

b.   'not complete'   _____

c.   'not significant'   _____

d.   'not relevant'   _____

e.   'not measurable'   _____

f.   'not modest'   _____

g.   'not legitimate'   _____

h.   'not mobile'   _____

i.   'not licit (legal)'   _____

j.   'not reverent'   _____

Part B Rewrite each sentence by replacing the prefix *en-* with its appropriate meaning. You may have to restructure some of the sentences.

Example:

    Please <u>ensure</u> that you sign your name to the application.

    Please <u>make certain</u> that you sign your name to the application.

a.   Human activities <u>endanger</u> animals all over the world.

    Human activities _____ animals _____ all over the world.

b.   The company *enlarged* its operation by 20 percent.

    The company _____ its operation _____ by 20 percent.

c.   Sally was <u>enraged</u> when her basketball team lost the game.

    Sally was _____ when her basketball team lost the game.

d.   Canadian culture has been <u>enriched</u> by immigrants.

    Canadian culture has been _____ by immigrants.

e.   The goal of feminism is to <u>empower</u> women.

    The goal of feminism is to _____ women _____.

UNIT 3

NOUN SUFFIXES

Pretest

      1. What is the difference between a suffix and a prefix?

      2. What does -ist in pianist mean?

      3. Give two meanings for -ism, as in criticism and Buddhism.

      4. What meaning does -ance, -ment and -ness share?

      5. What is a noun?

Definition: A **suffix** is something that is added to the end of a word, adds meaning, and indicates grammatical function.

English has many suffixes that are used to modify existing words. In this unit you will learn some of the most common noun suffixes, that is, suffixes that designate the grammatical function of a noun. Although these suffixes all designate nouns, they have a variety of different meanings.

Goals

- One goal is to build longer words by adding suffixes to familiar words.
- Another goal is to understand unfamiliar words by analyzing them as familiar words with suffixes.
- A third goal is to introduce parts of speech, starting with the noun, so that you can use English nouns in grammatical sentences.

Examples

Familiar Word	Suffixed Word	Meaning
kind	kindness	'the state of being kind'
good	goodness	'the state of being good'

Unit 3

| talk | talker | 'one that talks' |
| walk | walker | 'one that walks' |

The suffix *-ness* in *kindness* and *goodness* means 'the state of (being)' and adds this meaning to the base words *kind* and *good*. Similarly, the suffix *-er* adds the meaning 'one that does (a specified action)' to the base word. Once you know the form, meaning, and grammatical function of common suffixes like these, you will be able to start analyzing more unfamiliar words, to remember their meanings more easily, and to use them correctly in sentences.

Nouns

A noun names a person, place, thing, or idea. For example, *Sally*, *Vancouver*, *tree*, *dog*, *car*, and *peace* are nouns. Nouns can be replaced by the appropriate pronouns, whereas other types of words cannot: *she* for *Sally*, *it* for *Vancouver*, *car*, and *peace*, etc. Nouns are a class of words that can be used with articles like *a*, *an*, *the*, *this*, *that* and with possessive pronouns like *my, his, our*. Nouns can also be singular or plural: *car* or *cars*.

Nouns occur in particular places in English sentences. Look at these examples:

Bob is kind. His <u>kindness</u> is obvious to all his friends.
You talk fast. You are a fast <u>talker</u>.

It is ungrammatical to say or write:

Bob is kind. His <u>kind</u> is obvious to all his friends.
You talk fast. You are a fast <u>talk</u>.

Kind and *talk* create ungrammatical sentences when they are used like this in the place of a noun. Only their corresponding nouns, *kindness* and *talker*, can be used here. In this unit, you will learn about creating nouns by adding a noun suffix like *-ness* or *-er*. You will also get practice in the exercises on where to use base words and their corresponding nouns.

Suffixes Referring to People

Examine the list of suffixes below and learn their meanings. Please note that some suffixes in Table 1 have more than one meaning. They also tend to refer to people, although some can also be used to refer to things; you will learn more on this later in the unit.

Table 1

Form	Meaning	Example
-an, -ian	'a native of'	Canadian 'a native of Canada'
	'a supporter, believer'	Christian 'a believer of Christ'
	'one that works with'	musician 'one that works with music'
-ee	'person that is, does'	standee 'a person that stands'
		appointee 'a person that is appointed'
-er	'one that does'	talker 'one that talks'
	'one that makes, works'	hatter 'one that makes hats'
		miner 'one that works in a mine'
	'a native of'	New Yorker 'a native of New York'
	'one that is'	foreigner 'one that is foreign'
-ese	'a native of'	Chinese 'a native of China'
-ie, -y	'a dear little one'	sonny 'a dear little son'
	'one that is'	cutie 'one that is cute'
-ist	'one that does'	cyclist 'one that cycles'
	'one that plays, makes'	guitarist 'one that plays a guitar'
		novelist 'one that makes a novel'
	'one that specializes in'	biologist 'one that specializes in biology'
	'one that advocates'	royalist 'one that advocates royalty'
-ite	'a native of'	Vancouverite 'a native of Vancouver'
-or	'one that does'	actor 'one that acts'
-ster	'one that makes'	songster 'one that makes songs'
	'one that participates'	gangster 'one that participates in gangs'
	'one that is'	youngster 'one that is young'

Exercises: Table 1

3.1 Create a word by attaching the appropriate suffix to the base word.

Example: 'one that walks'   <u>walker</u>

a. 'one that specializes in geology'   _____

b. 'one that reads'   _____

c. 'one that is old'   _____

d. 'one that plays a violin'   _____

e. 'one that is sweet'   _____

f. 'one that participates in games'   _____

g. 'a native of Italy'   _____

h. 'a dear little girl'   _____

i. 'one that specializes in journalism'   _____

j. 'one that makes pots'   _____

k. 'a person that is absent'   _____

l. 'one that works with comedy'   _____

3.2 Give the meaning of the following words.

Example: banker   'one who works in a bank'_____

a. motorist   _____

b. European   _____

c. glover   _____

d. Brooklynite   _____

e. sailor   _____

f. Vietnamese   _____

Unit 3   31

g.   counselor   _____

h.   punster   _____

i.   escapee   _____

j.   electrician   _____

3.3 Fill the blank with the appropriate word from each pair of words provided. One word of the pair is a noun; the other is not. Here is a reminder about how to identify nouns and where to use them:

Nouns

- can be preceded by *a*, *an* or *the* (*a* dog, *an* apple, *the* car)
- can be singular or plural (car, car*s*)
- can be replaced by a pronoun (The man sings. *He* sings.)
- can be preceded by possessive pronouns (*his* car, *her* car, *their* car)

Example: makes, maker

Hyundai is a <u>maker</u> of automobiles.

Hyundai <u>makes</u> automobiles.

a.   act, actor

        John will _____ in Hamlet.

        John is an _____ in a Shakespearean play.

b.   sings, singer

        A _____ must have voice training if he or she wants to succeed.

        Pavarotti _____ in many different languages.

c.   cycle, cyclist

I want to _____ around the island.

The _____ went around the island.

d.   golfed, golfers

Fred and Amy _____ 18 holes every day of their holiday.

Fred and Amy are enthusiastic _____.

e.   employ, employees

The _____ listened very carefully to their supervisor.

The company will _____ ten more workers.

Suffixes Referring to Things

The suffixes in Table 2 are commonly used to refer to things. Two of them, -er and -ie, -y can refer to people as well, as you learned in the material above.

Table 2

Form	Meaning	Example
-dom	'office, realm, status'	earldom 'the office of an earl'
-er	'thing that does'	tape recorder 'a thing that records'
-ery	'a place for'	cannery 'a place for canning things'
-hood	'period (time)'	adulthood 'the period of being an adult'
-ie, -y	'a dear little thing'	birdie 'a dear little bird'
-ism	'doctrine'	Buddhism 'the doctrine of Buddha'
-ship	'office, skill'	dictatorship 'the office of a dictator'

Nouns ending with *-ie* or *-y* 'a dear little thing' are typically used in informal speech; that is, English speakers use them when they are talking to family or friends. You may want to avoid using such nouns in the more formal speech of the business world or of university life.

Exercises: Table 2

3.4 Fill in the blanks.

Example: 'a dear little bird'   <u>birdie</u>

a.   'period of being a child'   _____

b.   'the thing that computes'   _____

c.   'the doctrine of being a catholic'   _____

d.   'a dear little dog'   _____

e.   'the status of a (movie) star'   _____

f.   'a thing that cooks'   _____

g.   'the doctrine of being liberal'   _____

h.   'the realm of the king'   _____

i.   'the skill of a sportsman'   _____

j.   'a place for baking'   _____

3.5 Give the meaning of each word.

Example: 'birdie'   <u>a dear little bird</u>

a.   workmanship   _____

b. boyhood _____

c. Darwinism _____

d. stardom _____

e. printer _____

f. nunnery _____

Abstract Nouns

English has a number of noun suffixes that indicate the act, process, state, quality or condition of something. These suffixes create words that are referred to as **abstract nouns**. Often the exact meaning of the suffix is a little vague, but the important thing for you to remember is that it designates a part of speech: the noun. For example, *-ness* in *gentleness* indicates that *gentleness* is a noun whose meaning is 'the state or quality of being gentle'. It refers to the abstract state or quality of being gentle.

Gentle and *gentleness* are closely related words, but remember that they are not interchangeable in sentences. *Gentleness* belongs to the grammatical class of nouns, and must be used in sentences where English grammar requires a noun. Look at the following examples:

Mary is a <u>gentle</u> person. She is <u>gentle</u>.
Mary shows <u>gentleness</u> every day. I like her <u>gentleness</u>.

You would not say or write this:

Mary is a <u>gentleness</u> person. She is <u>gentleness</u>.
Mary shows <u>gentle</u> every day. I like her <u>gentle</u>.

This is ungrammatical English. You can see that it is important to learn how to use words correctly, in both their meaning and their grammar. Many nouns can be easily recognized by the suffix attached to the word. You will learn more about the proper use of nouns and other classes of words in this unit and throughout the textbook.

Table 3

Form	Meaning	Example
-age	'act, process, result'	breakage 'the act of breaking'
-ance	'act, state'	performance 'the act of performing'
-ation	'act, process'	flirtation 'the act of flirting'
-dom	'state'	freedom 'state of being free'
-ery, -ry	'state, condition, activity'	slavery 'the state of being a slave' rivalry 'the condition of being a rival'
-hood	'state, quality, shared state'	motherhood 'the state of being a mother
-ing	'act, process, result'	smoking 'to smoke (cigarettes)'
-ion	'act, state, result'	regulation 'the result of regulating'
-ism	'act, state'	criticism 'the act of a critic'
-ity, -ty	'state, quality, degree'	stupidity 'the state of being stupid' loyalty 'the state of being loyal'
-ment	'act, state'	amazement 'the state of being amazed'
-ness	'state, condition'	goodness 'the state of being good'
-ship	'state, condition'	friendship 'the state of being friends'
-th	'state, condition'	truth 'the state of being true'

Note that the final silent *e* of a base word like *regulate* is removed when a suffix is added: *regulation*. Also, base words ending in a *y* like *rely* will be spelled with an *I* when a suffix is added: *reliance*.

Exercises: Table 3

3.6 For each base word, add the suffix shown and make any required spelling adjustments.

Example: regulate (-ion)   <u>regulation</u>

a. distribute (-ion)   _____

b. embody (-ment)   _____

c. defy (-ance)   _____

d. compute (-ation)   _____

e. confuse (-ion)   _____

f. friendly (-ness)   _____

3.7 Add the appropriate suffix to the base word.

a. 'the state of being a martyr' (-dom)   _____

b. 'the shared state of being
    brothers' (-hood)   _____

c. 'the act or state of managing' (-ment)   _____

d. 'to ski' (-ing)   _____

e. 'the state of being rigid' (-ity)   _____

f. 'the state of being sad' (-ness)   _____

g. 'the activity of robbing' (-ery)   _____

h. 'the condition of growing' (-th)   _____

i. 'the state of being fellows' (-ship)   _____

j.   'the act of constructing' (-ion)   _____

k.   'the act or process of covering' (-age) _____

l.   'the act or state of being cruel' (-ty) _____

3.8 Determine which is the noun in each pair of words.

Example: true   truth   <u>truth</u>

a.   strong   strength   _____

b.   length   long   _____

c.   dirty   filth   _____

d.   death   die   _____

e.   broad   breadth   _____

f.   health   heal   _____

3.9 Write sentences for each pair of words, modeling your sentences on the examples given.

        Example: gentle, gentleness

        Models: <u>Margaret is a gentle person</u>.

                   <u>People notice her gentleness</u>.

a.   good, goodness

_____

_____

b.   sad, sadness

_____

_____

c.   friendly, friendliness

_____

_____

3.10 Fill the blank with the appropriate word from each pair of words provided. One word of the pair is a noun; the other is not.

Nouns

- can be preceded by *a*, *an* or *the* (*a* dog, *an* apple, *the* car)
- can be singular or plural (car, car*s*)
- can be replaced by a pronoun (The man sings. *He* sings.)
- can be preceded by possessive pronouns (*his* car, *her* car, *their* car)

Example: kind, kindness

Mary is <u>kind</u>.

People appreciate the <u>kindness</u> of strangers.

a.   hard, hardness

Diamonds are _____.

The _____ of diamonds is well known.

b.   boredom, bore

Frank and Betty _____ me.

Bill spent a long day of _____ at the office.

c.   argue, argument

Bob and Sheila are having an _____.

They _____ all the time.

d.   eat, eating

We _____ supper at 6 P.M.

Their _____ of supper was interrupted by a visitor.

e.   attendance, attend

My parents will _____ the meeting with the principal.

Their _____ at the meeting was noticed.

f.   Form, formation

The _____ of the Hawaiian Islands was due to volcanoes.

Volcanoes can _____ mountains.

g.   ship, shipment

We will _____ the goods to you on Friday.

The _____ will arrive in the afternoon.

h.   true, truth

The motto of *X-Files* is 'The _____ is out there.'

My sister is a _____ friend.

i.   confusion, confuse

All the _____ resulted from the robbery.

This problem will _____ you.

j.   acidity, acid

Vinegar has an _____ taste.

The _____ of this wine is overpowering.

k.   spoil, spoilage

The _____ of the food for the picnic was due to the very hot weather.

Food will _____ quickly in hot weather.

l.   brave, bravery

The soldier received a medal for his _____.

_____ soldiers receive medals.

Post-test

Part A Choose the most appropriate meaning for the suffix in each word.

Example: pianist   'one that plays the piano'

a.   heroism   _____

b.   craftsmanship   _____

c.   archeologist   _____

d.   trickster   _____

e.   dolly   _____

Part B Underline the **abstract** nouns that are recognizable by their suffixes in the following sentences.

Example: Many young people are tempted by drugs. The <u>temptation</u> to take drugs among teenagers is unfortunately very high.

a.   Some athletes can endure a lot of pain. The endurance of Olympic athletes is well-known. However sportsmanship among amateur athletes is better than among Olympic athletes.

b.   Volcanoes can erupt without much warning. Their eruptions cause devastation, hardship and disruption for people living near them.

c.   My older brother dissolved his partnership in the company; he left to join the priesthood. My younger brother is studying dentistry.

Part C Divide each word into the base word, the prefix and the suffix. Give a

Unit 3   42

meaning for the prefix and suffix.

a.   deforestation: prefix   _____

base word   _____

suffix   _____

b.   encirclement: prefix   _____

base word   _____

suffix   _____

c.   inaction: prefix   _____

base word   _____

suffix   _____

UNIT 4

VERBAL SUFFIXES

Pretest

1. What are the major suffixes used to create verbs in English

2. What is the meaning of the suffix *-ize* in *centralize*?

3. Does *-ize* have the same meaning in *hospitalize* as in *centralize*?

4. What is a verb?

5. What is the abstract noun corresponding to *simplify*?

In this unit you will learn about suffixes that attach to words to create verbs. In contrast to the many noun suffixes, there are only four common verbal suffixes.

Goals

- One goal is to build verbs by adding suffixes to familiar words.
- Another goal is to understand unfamiliar words by analyzing them as familiar words with suffixes.
- A third goal is to introduce parts of speech, continuing with the verb, so that you can use English words grammatically.

Verbs

A verb is a word that is required in any grammatical English sentence. It forms the core of the sentence and relates other words within the sentence to each other. Verbs typically express actions, occurrences, and states of being. Here are some examples:

The man <u>ate</u> the food.	(action)
The children <u>have played</u> tennis.	(action)
The moon <u>is shining</u> brightly.	(occurrence)
I <u>feel</u> hungry.	(state of being)

Unit 4   44

We <u>like</u> ice-cream.   (state of being)

You can recognize a verb in English in various ways:

1. The verb in the present tense must agree with its subject.

Singular	**Plural**
I *walk* the dog.	We *walk* the dog
You *walk* the dog.	You *walk* the dog.
She *walks* the dog.	They *walk* the dog.
The woman *walks* the dog.	The men *walk* the dog.

If the subject is singular and can be replaced by *he*, *she* or *it*, then the verb must have an -s ending.

2. Verbs indicate tense (past, present, future).

I *will go* to school tomorrow.	I *will talk* to you tomorrow.
I *went* to school yesterday.	I *talked* to you yesterday.

3. Verbs are often accompanied by auxiliary or helping verbs (*be*, *have*, *do* etc.).

He *is going* to the hockey game tonight.
We *have spoken* to you parents about your behavior.
Do you *have* her phone number?

Use these tips to help locate the verb in a sentence.

Verbal Suffixes

Many English verbs have been formed by adding one of four common suffixes to an existing word. You can improve your knowledge and familiarity of English verbs considerably by memorizing these suffixes and their meanings.

Table 1

Form	Meaning	Example
-ate	'make, cause, become'	validate 'to make valid'
-en	'make, cause'	lengthen 'to cause to have length, to make long'
-ify, -fy	'make, make similar to'	simplify 'to make simple' citify 'to make similar to a city'
-ize	'make' 'put into' 'become, make' 'engage in'	centralize 'to make central' hospitalize 'to put into hospital' Americanize 'to become (make) American' philosophize 'to engage in philosophy'

Remember the spelling rules when suffixes are attached to existing words. A silent *e* at the end of a base word is removed, and a final *y* becomes *I*:

Example: simple + -ify   <u>simplify</u>

city + -fy   <u>citify</u>

Exercises: Table 1

4.1 Give the meaning of the following words

Example   whiten   <u>'to make white'</u>

a.   familiarize   _____

b.   toughen   _____

c.   purify   _____

d.   activate   _____

e.   soften   _____

4.2 Create a verb by attaching the appropriate suffix to the base word.

Example: 'to make white' (-en)   <u>whiten</u>

a.   'to make into a union' (-ize)   _____

b.   'to make solid' (-ify)   _____

c.   'to make intense' (-ify)   _____

d.   'to provide with a motive' (-ate)   _____

e.   'to cause to be an alien' (-ate)   _____

f.   'to provide with decor' (-ate)   _____

g.   'to provide with beauty' (-ify)   _____

h.   'to make red' (-en)   _____

i.   'to become Italian' (-ize)   _____

j.   'to put into italics' (-ize)   _____

4.3 Add a suffix to the base word to create the verb in each sentence.

Example: Darkness <u>makes</u> the sky <u>black</u>. (-en)

                Darkness <u>blackens</u> the sky.

a.   The setting sun <u>makes</u> the sky <u>red</u>. (-en)

        The setting sun _____ the sky.

b.   Don't <u>make</u> your culture too <u>American</u>. (-ize)

        Don't _____ your culture too much.

Unit 4   47

c. The army put the citizens into terror. (-ize)

The army _____ the citizens.

d. Lady Gaga's wonderful singing held the audience captive. (-ate)

Lady Gaga's wonderful singing _____ the audience.

e. Spices make the flavor of food more intense. (-ify)

Spices _____ the flavor of food.

f. John's face went red with embarrassment. (-en)

John's face _____ with embarrassment.

g. English students must learn to use a hyphen correctly. (-ate)

English students must learn to _____ correctly.

h. A lot of money has been spent to make the Panama Canal deeper. (-en)

A lot of money has been spent to _____ the Panama Canal.

i. Teenagers often treat pop stars like idols. (-ize)

Teenagers often _____ pop stars.

j. Big dogs will tend to give small children a fright. (-en)

Big dogs will tend to _____ small children.

Unit 4

4.4 Fill the blank with the appropriate word from each pair of words provided. One word of the pair is a verb; the other is not. Here is a reminder about verbs:

Verbs

- agree with subjects in the present tense (He *walks*.)
- show tense (We *walked*. We ***will*** *walk*.)
- are often accompanied by auxiliaries (She *is going* to the movie.)

Example: broad, broadened

The city <u>broadened</u> the road last month.

The road is now <u>broad</u>.

a.   tender, tenderize

The _____ steak tasted good.

The steak will _____ in the mustard marinade.

b.   bright, brightens

The sun _____ this area of the garden in the late afternoon.

The _____ sun hurt my eyes.

c.   final, finalize

The _____ exam was given on the last day of class.

The businessmen will _____ the deal on Friday.

d.   valid, validate

Please _____ your ticket with the parkade supervisor.

You need a _____ ticket to park here.

e. hospital, hospitalized

We visited my sister-in-law in the _____.

She was _____ on Monday.

f. institution, institutionalizes

Society _____ violent criminals.

Prisons are one type of _____.

Verbs with Corresponding Nouns

Verbs that end in *-ate*, *-ify*, and *-ize* have corresponding abstract nouns. These

nouns are formed by adding a suffix to the verb. If you know the meaning of the verb, then you can easily determine the meaning of the corresponding abstract noun.

Table 2

Verb	Noun	Examples
-ate	-ation	validate, validation
-ify	-ification	simplify, simplification
-ize	-ization	centralize, centralization

Abstract nouns are formed by adding a noun suffix to the verb. For example, *validation* has *-ion* attached to the verb *validate*. Notice that the silent *e* is dropped in *-ate* when *-ion* is attached to it. The verb *validate* in turn is created by adding *-ate* to the base word *valid*. You can now see that both verbs and abstract nouns can be formed by adding suffixes to a base word. Sometimes a series of suffixes is attached:

Unit 4

```
valid + ate + ion            =    validation
central + ize + ate + ion    =    centralization
```

Validation means 'the action of making valid'. *Centralization* means 'the action of making central, the state of having been made central'.

Exercises: Table 2

4.5 Make abstract nouns from the verbs, and determine the base word upon which both the noun and the verb have been formed.

		Abstract noun	**Base word**
Example:	simplify	simplification	simple
a.	motivate	_____	_____
b.	intensify	_____	_____
c.	decorate	_____	_____
d.	civilize	_____	_____
e.	purify	_____	_____
f.	liberalize	_____	_____

4.6 Fill in the blank with the appropriate verb or noun.

	Verb	Noun
Example:	dictate	dictation
a.	complicate	_____
b.	_____	salivation

c.   regulate   _____

d.   calculate   _____

e.   _____   mediation

f.   _____   rotation

g.   meditate   _____

h.   _____   location

i.   investigate   _____

j.   populate   _____

4.7 Fill the blank with the appropriate word from each pair of words provided. One word of the pair is a verb; the other is a noun.

Example: simplify, simplification

Please <u>simplify</u> the exercise on page 22.

The <u>simplification</u> of the exercise will help all the students.

a.   civilized, civilization

The Romans _____ the Germans.

But the Roman _____ was eventually destroyed by German tribes.

b.   motivates, motivation

Some students lack _____.

The pursuit of a high grade _____ most students.

c.   familiarize, familiarization

_____ yourself with the text.

_____ with the text will help you pass the final examination.

d.   purifies, purification

The city of Vancouver _____ its drinking water.

Water _____ is important in maintaining good health.

e.   idolized, idolization

The _____ of movie stars is widespread among teenagers.

My wife has _____ Elvis since his death.

Post-test

Part A Give the meaning of the following words.

Example: weaken   'to make weak'

a.   Canadianize   _____

b.   publicize   _____

c.   lighten   _____

d.   captivate   _____

e.   diversify   _____

Part B Underline any verbs that have the suffixes introduced in this unit.

Example: Disease <u>weakens</u> plants. Weak plants often die.

a.   Fertile fields produce lots of crops. Farmers must therefore fertilize their fields.

b.   On Halloween the children got a big fright. Dressed as a ghost, Sarah frightened them to tears. Sarah's mother penalized her by making her stay inside for the rest of the night.

c.   Buttons will activate an elevator. An active elevator goes up and down; however, sudden stops and starts will roughen the ride for passengers.

Part C Choose the correct word to complete each sentence. Your choices include the base word, the verb and the noun.

Example: weak, weaken, weakness.

Disease <u>weakens</u> plants.

<u>Weak</u> plants often die.

Their <u>weakness</u> kills them.

a.   thick, thicken, thickness

You can _____ a sauce by adding cornstarch.

My grandfather spoke with a _____ Irish accent.

The sauce's _____ was just right.

b.   deep, deepened, deepness

Engineers measured the _____ of the lake.

His voice _____ when he reached fifteen.

This lake is _____.

c.   sterile, sterilize, sterilization

Doctors use _____ needles for injections.

The _____ of needles is necessary.

Surgeons _____ their hands before surgery.

UNIT 5

ADJECTIVAL SUFFIXES

Pretest

1. What is the meaning of *–ish in Swedish?*

2. What are some of the other major meanings of *-ish*?

3. Does *–ful* have the same meaning in *cupful* as in *hopeful*?

3. What is an adjective?

In this unit you will learn about suffixes that attach to existing words to create adjectives. Some English adjectival suffixes have a unique meaning, and many others share more or less the same meaning.

Goals:

- One goal is to build adjectives by adding suffixes to familiar words.
- Another goal is to understand unfamiliar words by analyzing them as familiar words with an adjectival suffix.
- A third goal is to introduce parts of speech, continuing with the adjective, so that you can use English words grammatically

Adjectives

An adjective describes nouns and pronouns; it adds information about them. Let's look at some examples.

He drives a <u>red</u> car.

She is <u>tall</u>.

A <u>large</u> dog appeared.

In the first example, the adjective *red* describes the noun *car*; in the second example, the adjective *tall* describes the pronoun *she*; and, in the final example, the adjective *large* describes the noun *dog*.

Adjectives in English tend to occur in certain positions in a sentence. You must know where to place them for you sentences to be grammatical. Here is a summary of the usual positions for adjectives.

1. Adjectives are usually placed before the noun they describe.

> A *red* car went past the house.

> The little girl wore *tiny* shoes.

> He has a *big* cat.

> The *burning* house sent smoke into the air.

2. Adjectives are often found after the forms of *be* (*be, am, are, is, was, were, been*):

> Be *good*!

> She is *tall*.

> The dog was *fat*.

> You are *sick*.

> They were *unhappy* about the outcome of the hockey game.

> You will be *rich* if you win today's lottery.

> Martha has been *quiet* all day.

3. Adjectives are often found after the linking verbs *appear, become, feel, grow, look, seem, smell, sound,* and *taste*. A linking verb links the noun or pronoun to an adjective:

> The roses smell *sweet*.

> The dog became *fat*.

Unit 5   57

He grew *old*.

The lemon tasted *sour*.

How do you know when a word like *grew* is being used as a linking verb?
Linking: My father *grew* tired.   (tired = adjective)

Nonlinking: My father *grew* potatoes. (potatoes = noun)

If the verb can be replaced by a form of *be*, then you know the verb is a linking verb. *My father grew tired* could be replaced with *My father was tired*, but you can't say *My father was potatoes*.

Adjectives of Origin and Location

In Unit 3 you learned that *-ese* and *-an* are suffixes that form nouns and that they describe a person who is a native or resident of a particular place. For instance, *Japanese* means 'person (or people) from Japan'. These two suffixes are also used to form adjectives, as in *a Japanese car* 'a car from Japan'. Another important suffix of origin is *-ish*. These three suffixes are tabled below.

Table 1

Form	Meaning	Example
-an, -ian	'of, relating to, from'	Canadian 'of, relating to, from Canada'
-ese	'of, relating to, from'	Chinese 'of, relating to, from China'
-ish	'of, relating to, from'	Swedish 'of, relating to Swedes or Sweden'

These adjectives refer to the place, the people, or their language depending on the context in which they are used.

The corresponding adjective for names of places ending in *-ia* is *-ian: Australia* becomes *Australian*. Very few examples are like *Canada*, which also takes the *-ian* form of the suffix.

Exercises: Table 1

5.1 Form adjectives from the following names for nationalities by attaching *-ish*, as shown in the example. Remember to drop the final silent *e* when adding the suffix to it.

	Country	**Person**	**Adjective**
Example:	Sweden	Swede	<u>Swedish</u>
a.	Turkey	Turk	_____
b.	Denmark	Dane	_____
c.	Finland	Finn	_____
d.	Scotland	Scot	_____
e.	Poland	Pole	_____
f.	Spain	Spaniard	_____
g.	Britain	Briton	_____
h.	England	Englishman	_____
i.	Ireland	Irishman	_____

5.2 Complete the sentences by using the appropriate suffix to create an adjective. You must put the adjective before the noun it describes.

Example: Businessmen <u>from China</u> met with Canadian officials. (-ese)

Chinese businessmen met with Canadian officials.

a.   Coffee <u>from Kenya</u> is exported to many places in the world. (-an)

_____ coffee is exported to many places in the world.

b.   I know a couple _from Canton_. (-ese)

I know a _____ couple.

c.   The Americans bombed the countryside _in Vietnam_ during the war. (-ese)

The Americans bombed the _____ countryside during the war.

d.   Jack became lost in the _mountains of Scotland_. (-ish)

Jack became lost in the _____.

e.   I don't know _the language of Burma_. (-ese)

I don't know_____ .

f.   These fossils are _from Morocco_. (-an)

These fossils are_____ .

g.   _The pyramids in Egypt_ have fascinated people for centuries. (-ian)

_____ have fascinated people for centuries.

h.   He was _from Malaysia_ and she was _from Africa_. (-an, -ian)

He was _____ and she was _____.

Some Common Adjectival Suffixes

In Table 2, some very common adjectival suffixes are listed. Two of these share the meaning 'like, resembling'; otherwise, the suffixes have different meanings.

Table 2

Form	Meaning	Example
-ing	'that does'	recording 'that records'
-less	'without'	helpless 'without help'
-like	'like, resembling'	childlike 'like, resembling a child'
-ly	'like, resembling'	saintly 'like, resembling a saint'
	'every'	hourly 'every hour'
-th	(used for numbers)	fourth 'number four in order'

Exercises: Table 2

5.3 Give the meaning of the following words.

Example: daily   'every day'

a.   blameless   _____

b.   lifelike   _____

c.   yearly   _____

d.   cowardly   _____

e.   fearless   _____

f.   warring   _____

5.4 Create an adjective by attaching the appropriate suffix to the base word.

Example: 'every day'   daily

a.   'number six in order'   _____

b.   'resembling a bird'   _____

c.   'without a child'   _____

Unit 5   61

d.   'every <u>week</u>'   _____

e.   'like a <u>father</u>'   _____

f.   'that <u>lasts</u>'   _____

g.   'without a <u>home</u>'   _____

h.   'without <u>noise</u>'   _____

5.5 Choose between the base word (noun or verb) and its corresponding adjective for each sentence.

Example: saint (noun), saintly

     Elizabeth has a <u>saintly</u> appearance.

     Elizabeth acts like a <u>saint</u>.

a.   endure (verb), enduring

     Poverty in the U.S. will _____ for many more years.

     Poverty is an _____ problem in the U.S.

b.   count (verb), countless

     We saw a _____ number of birds on the beach.

     We couldn't _____ the number of birds on the beach.

c.   wolf (noun), wolflike

     The Eskimo dog of the Canadian North is _____.

     The hikers saw a _____ in the forest.

Unit 5

d.	month (noun), monthly

Jackie gets paid once a _____.

Her _____ paycheck is spent on rent, bills and food.

e.	seven (adjective), seventh (number seven in order)

Bob has _____ cars.

He bought his _____ car last year.

f.	friends (noun), friendless

A _____ person has no _____.

5.6 Replace the underlined words by adding the appropriate suffix to the base words to create an adjective. Put the adjective in its correct grammatical position within the sentence.

Example:	Bill and Susan Murray are a couple <u>without children</u>.

Bill and Susan Murray are a <u>childless</u> couple.

a	Many people still think that O. J. Simpson is <u>without guilt</u> in the murder of his wife.

Many people still think that O. J. Simpson is _____ in the murder of his wife.

b.	The children saw an image <u>in the graveyard</u>.

The children saw a _____ image in the graveyard.

c.	<u>Plants that heal</u> are used throughout the world.

_____ are used throughout the world.

d.   Jack was in the <u>position of number twenty</u> in the long lineup for tickets.

Jack was in the _____ in the long lineup for tickets.

e.   These plants have <u>flowers shaped like bells</u>.

These plants have _____.

Suffixes with Similar Meanings

The next group of adjectival suffixes have confusingly similar meanings and are roughly synonymous. Their exact meanings are sometimes a little vague, but it is important to recognize the words as adjectives, and to use them correctly.

Table 3

Form	Meaning	Example
-able	'capable of, fit for, tending to'	teachable 'capable of being taught'
-al, -ar	'of, relating to'	autumnal 'relating to autumn' polar 'relating to a geographic pole'
-ative	'of, relating to, tending to'	talkative 'tending to talk'
-ed	'having, characterized by, like'	bearded 'having a beard'
-ful	'full of, tending to, like, filling'	fearful 'full of fear'
-ic	'of, relating to, like'	heroic 'like a hero'
-ical	'of, relating to, like'	theatrical 'of the theatre'
-ish	'like, relating to, tending to' 'about' 'somewhat'	brutish 'like a brute' noonish 'about noon' reddish 'somewhat red'
-ive	'tending to, making'	active 'tending to act'
-ous	'having, possessing, full of'	cancerous 'full of cancer'
-y	'full of, like, tending to'	hairy 'full of hair'

Unit 5

The two forms -al and -ar are really the same sufffix: -ar is used if an l is located somewhere before the suffix (lunar, solar); otherwise, -al is typically used.

The suffixes -ic and -ical (a combination of -ic + al) often form adjectives with the same meaning: metaphoric and metaphorical both mean 'like a metaphor'.

Note also that -ful and -less are **antonyms**: they are opposite in meaning:

fearful 'full of fear'   fearless 'without fear'

Exercises: Table 3

5.7 Give the meaning of the following words.

Example: acidic   'of acid, relating to acid'

a.   agreeable   _____

b.   sleepy   _____

c.   glorious   _____

d.   educated   _____

e.   childish   _____

f.   brownish   _____

g.   natural   _____

h.   qualitative   _____

i.   abusive   _____

j.   pitiful   _____

k.   cupful   _____

l.   satanic   _____

Unit 5   65

m. geometrical   _____

n. molecular   _____

5.8 Create an adjective by attaching the appropriate suffix to the base word. The suffix is given to you only in those cases where the meaning matches more than one suffix.

Example: 'relating to acid' (-ic)   <u>acidic</u>

a. 'filling a mouth'   _____

b. 'somewhat black'   _____

c. 'tending to assert' (-ive)   _____

d. 'relating to medicine (-al)   _____

e. 'tending to itch' (-y)   _____

f. 'capable of being worked'   _____

g. 'like a baby' (-ish)   _____

h. 'about fifty'   _____

5.9 Choose between the base word (noun or verb) and its corresponding adjective for each sentence.

Example: beard (noun), bearded

        Michael has a <u>beard</u>.

        The <u>bearded</u> man is Michael.

a. metal (noun), metallic

        Copper is a _____.

Unit 5

This chair is _____.

b. hope (noun), hopeful

The politician is full of _____ about the next election.

She is _____ that she will win.

c. girl, girlish

Susan's _____ smile charms everyone.

Susan has two children: a _____ and a boy.

d. dirt (noun), dirty

Jack sweeps the _____ under the carpet.

He also leaves the _____ dishes in the sink.

e. fade (verb), faded

The _____ newspapers lay in the street.

Newspapers will _____ if they are in the sun.

f. employ (verb), employable

Businesses like to _____ trained people.

Trained people are _____.

g. season (noun), seasonal

Picking apples is _____ work.

Unit 5

Autumn is a colorful _____.

h.   selected (verb), selective

My wife _____ some paint for the house.

You have to be _____ as a consumer in today's society.

5.10 Replace the underlined words by adding the appropriate suffix to the base words to create an adjective. Put the adjective in its correct grammatical position within the sentence.

Example: The man <u>with the beard</u> is Michael.

The <u>bearded</u> man is Michael.

a.   Mary is <u>about thirty</u>.

Mary is _____.

b.   His clothes <u>like rags</u> appalled everyone. (-ed)

His _____ clothes appalled everyone.

c.   Pigs aren't <u>full of fur</u>. (-y)

Pigs aren't _____.

d.   His <u>office that has lots of space</u> holds lots of people. (-ious)

His _____ holds lots of people.

e.   My uncle is <u>somewhat old</u>.

      My uncle is _____.

f.   Byron is a <u>poet full of mystery</u>. (-ious)

      Byron is a _____.

g.   We want a <u>worker that we can rely on</u>. (-able)

      We want a _____.

Post-test

Part A Divide each word into the base word and suffix, and then give the meaning of the whole word.

Example: famous   <u>fame + ous 'having fame'</u>

a.   nightly   _____

b.   exhaustive   _____

c.   fictional   _____

d.   Nepalese   _____

e.   bigoted   _____

Part B Choose the correct word for each sentence.

Example: brute, brutish

            Some humans engage in <u>brutish</u> behavior.

            May called her husband a <u>brute</u> because he bullied her sister.

Unit 5   69

a. grace   graceless   graceful

She shows much _____ when she dances.

After years of practice, ballerinas are _____ dancers.

Someone without grace is _____.

b. rest   restless   restful

The Robinson family spent a _____ Sunday afternoon   watching videos.

Children need their _____.

My brother spent a _____ night in the hospital because it was so noisy.

c. real   realist realistic

Bob was _____ about his job opportunities.

Sarah has a ring with _____ diamonds.

Bob is a _____ about his job opportunities.

Part C Choose a synonym (i.e., a word of similar meaning) for each word from the list.

Example: graceless   <u>clumsy</u>

Synonyms: quiet, clumsy, uncertain, uneasy, crying, expectant, unafraid, happy, easy.

Unit 5

a.   restless   _____

b.   noiseless   _____

c.   doubtful   _____

d.   fearless   _____

e.   joyful   _____

f.   tearful   _____

g.   effortless   _____

h.   hopeful   _____

UNIT 6

BOUND FORMS WITH NOUN AND VERBAL SUFFIXES

Pretest

1. What is meant by a bound form?

2. What is the meaning of the suffix *–ee* in nominee?

3. Does the suffix *–or* have the same meaning in *doctor* as in *tractor*?

4. Which to of the four verb suffixes are commonly found in bound forms?

In this unit you will learn about bound forms, that is, forms that occur with a prefix or suffix but that do not exist by themselves as English words.

Goals

- One goal is to learn about bound forms in English.
- Another goal is to understand unfamiliar words by analyzing them as bound forms with common suffixes.
- A third goal is to memorize the meanings of bound forms so that you will recognize them in other English words.

Bound Forms

In the previous units you learned about creating words by adding prefixes and suffixes to existing words. Because existing words can stand by themselves as independent words they are called free or unbound forms. For example, *work* is a free form; that is, it can stand on its own as a word to which you can add prefixes and suffixes: *rework* and *workable*.

On the other hand, **bound forms** are forms that can only occur with prefixes or suffixes; they do not exist as independent words by themselves. Two examples are *repel* 'to drive back' and *capable* 'able to do things well'. You can easily recognize the prefix and the suffix in these words, but notice that *pel* and *cap* (here meaning 'take') do not exist as English words. They do have meaning, however, and these are the word parts that we call bound forms.

In the word *dentist* you should be able to recognize the suffix *-ist* 'one that specializes in', but you may not recognize the bound form *dent* 'teeth'. Of course *dentist* means 'one that specializes in teeth'. Although *dent* 'teeth' cannot occur by itself in English, it does have a specific meaning and recurs with this meaning in several words:

> dental 'of or relating to teeth'
> denture 'a set of false teeth'
> dentate 'having teeth'
> dentifrice 'substance for cleaning the teeth'
> edentate 'lacking teeth'

Since English has a large number of bound forms, it is good to recognize some of the more common ones because such recognition helps you to develop your vocabulary. You will be able to analyze and guess at the meaning of an unfamiliar word if you can recognize the bound form and its suffix.

Most of the bound forms of English have come into the language from Latin and Greek over the centuries.

Noun Suffixes Referring to People and Things

Here are some common suffixes that occur with bound forms. You have seen them before, as they also attach to existing words to create nouns.

Table 1

Form	Meaning	Example
-ee	'one that is or receives'	nominee 'one that is named'
-er	'one that does'	barber 'one that cuts hair'
-ist	'one that does'	dramatist 'one that writes plays'
	'one that specializes in'	chemist 'one that specializes in chemistry'

-or	'one that does'	doctor 'one that practices medicine'
	'thing that does'	tractor 'machine that pulls'

The word *nominee* is analyzed as follows:

nomin 'name, named' + -ee 'one that is'   'one that is named'

The bound form has the meaning 'name, named', and the suffix adds its own meaning and grammatical function to create the noun *nominee*. Make sure you memorize each bound form as you encounter it in the tables and in the exercises.

Exercises: Table 1

6.1 Create a word by attaching the appropriate suffix to the bound form. The bound forms are listed below.

nomin 'name, named'   flor 'flower'
don 'give, gift'   spons 'support'
ocul 'eye'   evacu 'removed'
hedon 'pleasure'   ment 'guide'
trait 'betray'

Example: 'one that is named' (-ee)   nominee

a.   'one that specializes in
      the eyes' (-ist)   _____

b.   'one that supports' (-or)   _____

c.   'one that receives a gift' (-ee)   _____

d.   'one that sells flowers' (-ist)   _____

e.   'one that is removed' (-ee)   _____

f.   'one that guides' (-or)   _____

Unit 6   74

g.   'one that enjoys pleasure' (-ist)   _____

h.   'one that betrays' (-or)   _____

6.2 Give the meaning of each word.

don 'give, gift'	applicat 'apply'	lingu 'language, tongue'
less 'lease'	cens 'examine'	impost 'deceive'
nomin 'named'	scient 'science'	

Example: nominee   <u>'one that is named'</u>

a.   linguist   _____

b.   lessee   _____

c.   donor   _____

d.   impostor   _____

e.   applicator   _____

f.   censor   _____

g.   scientist   _____

Suffixes Referring to Abstract Nouns

Again, you have seen some of these suffixes before; however, some are new.
You will learn more bound forms in Table 2 and in the corresponding exercises.

Table 2

Form	Meaning	Example
-age	'act, state, result'	courage 'the state of being brave'
-ion	'act, state, result'	junction 'the state of being joined'

Unit 6   75

-ism	'act, state'	barbarism 'the state of being a barbarian'
-itude	'act, state, quality'	certitude 'the state of being certain'
-ity, -ty	'state, quality, degree'	ability 'the quality of being able'
-ure	'act, state, result'	tenure 'the act or state of holding'

You can now see that a word like *courage* is analyzable as *cour*, which means 'brave', and the noun-forming suffix -*age*. Similarly, *ten* in *tenure* means 'hold', and the -*ure* suffix makes it into a noun referring to the act or state of holding.

Exercises: Table 2

6.3 Give the meaning of the underlined base form.

Example: junction 'the state of being joined'   join

a.   gratitude 'the action of thanking'   _____

b.   charity 'the state or condition of love
       (for the poor or suffering)'   _____

c.   salvage 'the action of saving'   _____

d.   union 'the state of being one'   _____

e.   dignity 'the state of having honor or pride'   _____

f.   multitude 'the state of being many'   _____

g.   advantage 'the state of having a
       superior position'   _____

h.   baptism 'the action of purifying in water'   _____

6.4 Fill the blank with the appropriate word from each pair of words provided.

Example: junction, join

Unit 6

The new highway will <u>join</u> the old highway at Kingston.

The <u>junction</u> of the new and old highways will be at Kingston.

a. salvage, saved

When the ship sank, all the sailors were _____.

The _____ washed upon the shore.

b. gratitude, thank

The child showed _____ for the many birthday gifts.

The child will _____ everyone who brought a gift.

c. leisure, free from work

It's nice to be _____.

Tony spends his _____ playing golf.

d. pull, tractor

The farmer uses his _____ to plough his corn field.

His truck is sometimes used to _____ wagons full of hay.

e. brave, courage

The _____ firefighter pulled the child out of the burning house.

The firefighter was given a medal for his _____.

f.   fortitude, strong

A _____ person can stay in the forest over night without being afraid.

Sally showed much _____ by staying in the forest alone for the whole night.

g.   honest, rectitude

The politician was noted for his _____.

Sometimes it's hard to find an _____ politician.

h.   latitude, free

The teacher gave the student _____ to do whatever he wanted.

The student was _____ to do whatever he wanted.

i.   mission, sent

The spy was given an impossible _____.

The agency _____ the spy to Lagos.

Verbal Suffixes

Two of the four verb suffixes learned in Unit 4 commonly occur with bound forms. You will find many verbs in English that consist of a bound form plus *-ate* or *-ify*.

Table 3

Form	Meaning	Example

Unit 6

-ate	'cause to become, make'	abbreviate 'to make short'
-ify, -fy	'make, become'	certify 'to make certain'

Exercises: Table 3

6.5 Create a word by attaching the appropriate suffix to the bound form. The bound forms are listed below.

educ 'schooled'	test 'witness'
ampl 'great, strong'	enumer 'list'
terr 'frightened'	cert 'certain'
calcul 'figure, estimate'	

Example: 'to make certain' (-ify)   <u>certify</u>

a.   'to make great or strong' (-ify)   _____

b.   'to make frightened' (-ify)   _____

c.   'to become schooled' (-ate)   _____

d.   'to become a witness' (-ify)   _____

e.   'to make a list, to count' (-ate)   _____

f.   'to figure out, to estimate' (-ate)   _____

6.6 Give the meaning of the underlined base form.

Example: <u>cert</u>ify 'to make certain'   <u>certain</u>

a.   <u>devi</u>ate 'to cause to turn aside
       (from a course, rule or truth)   _____

b.   <u>putre</u>fy 'to cause to rot'   _____

c.   <u>consecr</u>ate 'to make sacred'   _____

Unit 6   79

d.   integrate 'to cause to be whole'   _____

e.   verify 'to prove to be true'   _____

f.   terminate 'to cause to end'   _____

g.   liquefy 'to make into a liquid'   _____

h.   dedicate 'to make a gift of'
       (for some serious purpose)   _____

i.   fortify 'to make strong'   _____

j.   rectify 'to make right'   _____

6.7 Choose the appropriate noun or verb for each sentence.

Example: certitude, certify

       The chartered account will certify the documents.

       John said with certitude that Barbara was at the party.

a.   gratitude, gratify

       Mr. Watson expressed _____ to those who attended his
       wife's funeral.

       It will _____ Mr. Watson that so many people attended
       his wife's funeral.

b.   dignity, dignify

       Do not _____ that silly question with an answer.

       A Prime Minister must show _____ when in office.

c.   baptism, baptize

Who will _____ the baby?

The _____ of the baby will take place next Sunday.

d.   fortitude, fortify

Climbers of Mount Everest must have great _____.

The good lunch will _____ them for the hike.

e.   rectitude, rectify

They will _____ the spelling mistakes before handing the
assignment in to the teacher.

Priests and ministers must show _____ at all times.

f.   union, unified

Canada is a _____ of provinces and territories.

During the last election the issue of unemployment
_____ the various parties.

g.   horror, horrify

Ghosts and goblins _____ children.

The _____ of seeing the thief made the children scream.

6.8 Choose the synonym (i.e., a word of similar meaning) from the list below that

Unit 6   81

matches each word.

Synonyms: rot, strengthen, stray, frighten, list, affirm, enlarge, shorten, give completely

Example: fortify   strengthen
                                         _____

a.   verify   _____

b.   abbreviate   _____

c.   amplify   _____

d.   deviate   _____

e.   dedicate   _____

f.   putrefy   _____

g.   enumerate   _____

h.   terrify   _____

Post-test

Part A Divide each word into the bound form and suffix, and then give the meaning of the bound form.

Example: doctor 'one that practices medicine'

            doct + or   'practice medicine'

a.   tailor 'one that sews (clothes)'

_____   _____

b.   arbiter 'one that decides (a dispute)'

_____   _____

c.   pacify 'to make calm'

_____   _____

d.   nominate 'to name'

_____   _____

e.   amplify 'to make great, strong'

_____   _____

f.   horror 'thing that frightens'

_____   _____

g.   celebrate 'to make merry'

_____   _____

h.   religion 'the action of worship'

_____   _____

i.   similitude 'the state of being similar'

_____   _____

j.   outrage 'an action that insults or offends'

_____   _____

Part B Look for the verb suffixes you've learned in this unit, and then select the verb in each pair.

Verb

Example: gratitude   gratify   <u>gratify</u>

a.   dedication   dedicate   _____

b.   arbiter   arbitrate   _____

c.   terminal   terminate   _____

d.   baptize   baptismal   _____

Part C Look for the noun suffixes you've learned in this unit, and then select the noun in each pair.

Noun

Example: gratitude   gratify   <u>gratitude</u>

a.   termination   terminal   _____

b.   creation   create   _____

c.   unity   unionize   _____

d.   similar   similitude   _____

Unit 6

UNIT 7

BOUND FORMS WITH ADJECTIVAL SUFFIXES

Pretest

    1. What is the meaning of *–ile* in *mobile*?

    2. What part of speech does *–ine* create in *feline*?

    3. What is the bound form of *horror* and *horrid*?

    4. What is the adjective corresponding to the noun *eternity*?

    5. What is the adjective corresponding to the verb *purify*?

In this unit you will learn about adjectival suffixes that attach to bound forms.

Goals:

- One goal is to learn more about bound forms in English.
- Another goal is to understand unfamiliar words by analyzing them as bound forms with common adjectival suffixes.

Adjectival Suffixes

Some of the adjectival suffixes in the following table are ones that you have seen before; however, some will be new to you.

Table 1

Form	Meaning	Example
-able, -ible	'capable of, fit for, tending to'	portable 'capable of being carried' visible 'capable of being seen'

-al, -ar	'of, relating to'	mortal 'relating to death'
		lunar 'relating to the moon'
-ic	'of, relating to, like'	civic 'relating to a city'
-id	'of, relating to'	horrid 'relating to horror'
-ile	'capable of, characteristic of'	mobile 'capable of moving'
-ine	'of, like, having the nature of'	canine 'like a dog'
-ous, -ious	'having, possessing, full of'	oblivious 'not having awareness'

Exercises: Table 1

7.1 Create a word by attaching the suffix provided to the bound form.

femin 'female'	nat 'birth'
rig 'hardness'	soci 'companionship'
hilar 'great fun'	sol 'sun'
trag 'tragedy'	juven 'young'
lun 'moon'	

Example: 'of the moon' (-ar)   <u>lunar</u>

a.   'relating to great fun' (-ious)   _____

b.   'relating to tragedy' (-ic)   _____

c.   'relating to hardness' (-id)   _____

d.   'fit for companionship' (-able)   _____

e.   'of the sun' (-ar)   _____

f.   'characteristic of the young' (-ile)   _____

g.   'having a female nature (-ine)   _____

h.   'of birth' (-al)   _____

7.2 Give the meaning of each word.

civ 'city'   matern 'mother'
tep 'warmth'   fert 'reproduction'
dras 'severity'   ranc 'rot'
flor 'flower'   delic 'good taste'
mut 'change'   fel 'cat'
mascul 'male'

Example: civic   <u>'relating to a city'</u>

a.   rancid   _____

b.   fertile   _____

c.   floral   _____

d.   mutable   _____

e.   drastic   _____

f.   feline   _____

g.   tepid   _____

h.   delicious   _____

i.   maternal   _____

j.   masculine   _____

7.3 Match each word with the correct synonym (i.e., a word of similar meaning) by using the bound roots as your guide.

frag 'break'   cred 'believe'   sal 'salt'   ted 'bore'
horr 'fear'   div 'god'   nox 'harm'   mar 'sea'
flu 'flow'   frig 'cold'   etern 'last always'

Example: saline   <u>salty</u>

breakable

a.   credible   _____   harmful

b.   divine   _____   everlasting

c.   frigid   _____   salty

d.   tedious   _____   cold

e.   horrible   _____   boring

f.   fragile   _____   flowing

g.   noxious   _____   sea

h.   eternal   _____   believable

i.   marine   _____   godly

j.   fluid   _____   fearful

7.4 Fill each blank with the correct noun or adjective. You will recognize the adjective by its suffix.

Example: dog, canine

a barking <u>dog</u>

a <u>canine</u> disease

a.   sea, marine

the deep blue _____

a _____ climate

Unit 7

The Mediterranean _____ is full of _____ life.

b.   sun, solar

the hot _____

a _____ eclipse

_____ panels store heat from the _____.

c.   mortal, death

a _____ injury

a slow _____

A _____ illness will cause _____.

d.   moon, lunar

a bright full _____

a _____ crater

In a _____ eclipse the earth comes between the sun and the

_____.

e.   flower(s), floral

a _____ decoration

the smell of a _____

A _____ pattern is made up of _____.

f.   manual, hands

the _____ worker

dirty _____

_____ labor means to labor with the _____.

7.5 Fill each blank with the correct word.

Example: fiction, fictional

The writer gave a <u>fictional</u> account of the Vietnam War.

D.H. Lawrence wrote <u>fiction</u> and poetry.

a.   eternal, eternity

The exam seemed to last for an _____.

Some people desire _____ life.

b.   superstition, superstitious

Some hockey players are very _____.

Some people claim there is a connection between religion and

_____.

c.   rigidity, rigid

_____ is the state of being stiff.

When I was a child, my mother had _____ rules about doing homework.

Unit 7

d. putrid, putrefy

They threw the _____ meat into the garbage.

Meat will _____ if left in the hot sun.

e. similarity, similar

The brothers are _____ in appearance.

The _____ of the twins is striking.

f. religion, religious

Some _____ people worship every day.

Islam is a major _____.

g. terminal, terminate

The company is going to _____ Mary's job.

Sue has a _____ disease.

h. outrage, outrageous

It is an _____ that politicians do not keep their election promises.

The teenager's _____ behavior shocked everyone.

i. oblivious, oblivion

Frank was _____ to the noise the children made in the backyard.

Some people seek _____ through drugs and alcohol.

j.   hilarity, hilarious

The comic's jokes caused great _____.

The _____ comic made everyone laugh.

Post-test

Part A Determine which of the pair contains the bound form.

Example: serpentine, canine   <u>canine</u>

a.   missile, projectile   _____

b.   glorious, serious   _____

c.   oral, regional   _____

d.   workable, horrible   _____

e.   polar, molar   _____

f.   acidic, caustic   _____

g.   elephantine, feline   _____

Part B Fill each blank with the correct word.

Example: grateful, gratitude, gratify

Your <u>gratitude</u> means a lot to me.

I am <u>grateful</u> for your help.
The candy will <u>gratify</u> the child's desire for something sweet.

Unit 7   92

a.   nominee, nominate, nominal

The politician only had _____ success, and soon became

unpopular.

The political _____ thanked all his supporters.

Will you _____ me for the committee?

b.   horror, horrify, horrid

The _____ accident left two people dead.

The _____ of the fire gave the children nightmares.

Nightmares about the fire _____ the children.

c.   terror, terrify, terrible

He made a _____ mistake when he left the keys in the car.

Terrorists use _____ to intimidate civilians.

Big dogs _____ small children.

UNIT 8

PATTERNS OF CORRESPONDENCES

Pretest

    1. What is the abstract noun corresponding to *capable*?

    2. Is *absent* a noun or an adjective?

    3. What is the adjective corresponding to *circle*?

    4. What is the abstract noun corresponding to *deceive*?

    5. What is the adjective corresponding to *permit*?

In this unit you will learn about particular patterns that link related words. These related words have similar meanings but belong to different parts of speech.

Goals:

- One goal is to learn the patterns that relate words to one another.
- Another goal is to create longer words by adding suffixes to an existing word.
- A third goal is to recognize the relationship between a base word and its corresponding bound form.

Correspondences

English has many words that are closely related to one another. You have already learned about many closely related words like *work - rework*, *red - redden*, and *horror - horrify*. Here you will learn about particular patterns that exist between pairs of words. For example, one common pattern exists between adjectives with the suffix *-able* and their corresponding nouns with suffix *-ability*:

    adjective: workable 'capable of being worked'
    abstract noun: workability 'the state of being workable'

By memorizing such common patterns, you will be able to enlarge your vocabulary.

Adjectives Ending in *-able* or *-ible* and Their Abstract Nouns

Many adjectives ending in *-able* have a corresponding abstract noun suffixed with *-ability*, which means 'state, condition, capacity, fitness, or tendency'. Likewise, the abstract noun corresponding to *-ible* ends with *-ibility*, and has the same meaning as *-ability*. Notice that these abstract noun suffixes were formed by adding *-ity* to *-able* and *-ible*. Although they are spelled differently, *-able* and *-ible* are pronounced the same, and so are *-ability* and *-ibility*.

Table 1

Adjective	Abstract Noun
obtainable 'capable of being obtained'	obtainability
changeable 'capable of change or being changed'	changeability
saleable 'easily sold, fit to be sold'	saleability (or salability)
visible 'capable of being seen'	visibility
flexible 'easily bent, easily adapted'	flexibility
admissible 'capable of being admitted, allowable'	admissibility

Exercises: Table 1

8.1 Providing the appropriate adjective or abstract noun

Example: teachable
'able to be taught, capable of being taught'

<u>teachability</u>

a.   readable
'enjoyable to read'

_____

b.   responsible
'deserving credit or blame, trustworthy, expected to account for'

_____

c.   portability
'capable of being moved about'

_____

d.   feasible
'capable of being done easily, likely'

_____

e.   reliability
'capable of being relied on'

_____

f.   credibility
'believable, trustworthy'

_____

g.   sociable
'friendly'

_____

h.   transferable
'capable of being transferred'

_____

i.   defensible
'capable of being defended, justifiable'

_____

j.   accessibility
         'capable of being reached, easy to enter'

         _____

k.   manageability
         'capable of being managed'

         _____

8.2 Complete the following sentences by providing the appropriate adjective or abstract noun.

Example: accessible 'capable of being reached'
           accessibility

         The lake was <u>accessible</u> from the nearby highway.

         The easy <u>accessibility</u> of the lake made it a popular picnic spot.

a.   readable 'enjoyable to read'
         readability

         The_____ of this book made it a best seller.

         People say that this book is very_____.

b.   credible 'believable'
         credibility

         Because Jacob had been in prison, people doubted his
         _____.

         The police thought that his story was not_____.

c.   reliable 'capable of being relied on'
    reliability

    May is a_____ worker.

    People traveling to work on the train depend on the
    _____ of the system.

d.   responsible 'expected to account for'
    responsibility

    You are_____ for your books.

    It is your_____ to look after your books.

e.   visible 'capable of being seen'
    visibility

    _____ was terrible because of the thick fog.

    The shore was barely_____ through the thick fog.

Adjectives Ending in *-ant* or *-ent* and Their Abstract Nouns

Many adjectives that are suffixed with *-ant* or *-ent* have a corresponding abstract noun ending in *-ance* or *-ence*. The adjective refers to 'performing (a certain action) or being (in a certain condition)', and often corresponds to the suffix *-ing*. The noun refers to the corresponding 'state, quality, or action'.

adjective: reliant 'relying, trusting'
abstract noun: reliance 'the action, state or quality of relying, trusting'

Table 2

Adjective	Abstract Noun
relevant 'bearing on the matter at hand'	relevance

defiant 'openly resisting, offering a challenge'   defiance
elegant 'having good taste, expressed with taste'   elegance
confident 'certain, sure of oneself'   confidence
different 'differing, not the same, distinct'   difference
patient 'bearing pains or trials calmly'   patience

No doubt you have noticed that adjectives ending in -ant have -ance as their corresponding abstract noun, whereas those ending in -ent have -ence as their noun.

Although the adjectival suffixes are spelled differently, they are pronounced the same, and the two abstract noun suffixes are also pronounced in the same way.

Exercises: Table 2

8.3 Fill in the blank by providing the appropriate adjective or abstract noun.

	Adjective	Abstract Noun
Example:	defiant 'resisting, offering a challenge'	defiance
a.	_____ 'controlling, ruling, strongest'	dominance
b.	_____ 'willing to obey'	obedience
c.	competent 'able, fit, adequate, sufficient'	_____
d.	resistant 'resisting'	_____
e.	_____ 'wealthy, lavish'	opulence

Unit 8   99

f. tolerant _____
   'tolerating'

g. present _____
   'not being absent,
   being or occurring now'

h. _____   importance
   'having value or significance, having
   influence'

i. absent _____
   'away, lacking, not existing'

j. brilliant _____
   'shining brightly, magnificent, having
   great ability'

8.4 Complete the following sentences by providing the appropriate adjective or abstract noun.

Example: present 'not absent'
          presence

          The teacher was <u>present</u> in the classroom when the student fainted.
          We require your <u>presence</u> at the next meeting.

a. absent 'away'
   absence

   The twins were _____ from school today.

   Their _____ was due to the flu.

b. obedient 'willing to obey'
   obedience

   Your dog's _____ is admirable.

Unit 8

Your dog is very _____.

c.   different 'differing, not the same'
      difference

      We want to try a _____ approach to this problem.

      One _____ between you and me is that I enjoy classical
      music and you don't.

d.   elegant 'expressed with taste'
      elegance

      What an _____ room this is!

      I like the _____ of this room.

e.   persistent 'persisting, lasting, continuing'
      persistence

      The _____ of the economic downturn in Asia bothered
      people worldwide.

      Raymond had a _____ headache that lasted for three
      days.

Nouns Ending in *-le* and Their Corresponding Adjectives Ending in *-ular*

Some nouns ending in the letters *-le* have a corresponding adjective that ends in
the sequence *-ular*.

      noun: circle
      adjective: circular 'of or relating to a circle'

The noun *circle* is an independent word, but its bound form *circul* occurs with the
adjectival suffix *-ar* 'of or relating to'. Bound forms like *circul* never occur by
themselves, but only in conjunction with a suffix.

Unit 8   101

Table 3

Noun	Adjective
circle	circular 'of or relating to a circle'
muscle	muscular 'of or relating to a muscle'
people	popular 'of the people, liked by many people'

The bound form that occurs with adjectives may occur in other parts of speech as well. For example, the bound form *circul* also occurs in the verb *circulate* 'to move
around in a circuit' and in the noun *circulation* 'movement in a circuit'.

Exercise: Table 3

8.5 Fill in the blank with the appropriate noun or adjective.

	Noun	Adjective
Example:	muscle	muscular 'of or relating to a muscle'

a. angle   _____
    'space between two lines'   'of or relating to an angle'

b. _____   singular
    'only one'   'the only one of its kind, unusual'

c. _____   spectacular
    'a public show or display'   'having to do with a show,
                                               making a great display'

d. title   _____
    'a name'   'having a title, in title or name only'
e. testicle   _____
    'male reproductive organ'   'of or relating to the testicles'

f. _____   triangular
    'a figure having three sides'   'of or relating to a three-sided figure'

8.6 Complete the definition for each of the following words by finding the corresponding noun *-le*.

Example: titular   'having a <u>title</u>, in name only'

a.   musculature 'a system of _____ s'

b.   population   'the whole number of _____ in a
                    country or region'

c.   rectangular 'shaped like a _____ '

d.   triangulate 'to divide into _____ s'

e.   populous   'inhabited by many _____ '

f.   circularity 'having the quality or form of a _____ '

g.   populace   'the _____ in general'

Verbs and Their Abstract Nouns Ending in *-tion*

Many verbs have a corresponding abstract noun that ends in *-tion*; this ending is a combination of *t* and the suffix *-ion*. You recall that *-ion* is a suffix that creates abstract nouns and has the meaning of 'act, state, result, condition, or process'. In some verbs, the final silent *e* is dropped when the noun suffix *-tion* is added. Verbs ending in *-duce* follow this pattern:

Loss of silent *e*:

Verb	Abstract Noun
produce 'to make'	production 'the act of producing'

In other verbs, the final silent *e* is dropped and a consonant change occurs when the noun suffix is added. Verbs ending in *-scribe* and *-ceive* follow this pattern:

Consonant change:

Verb	Abstract Noun
describe 'to tell or write about'	description 'the act of describing'
perceive 'to be aware through the senses'	perception 'the act of perceiving'

The consonant *b* in *describe* appears as *p* in *description*; the consonant *v* in *perceive* appears as *p* in *perception*.

Another set of verbs adds a consonant to the base word when the abstract noun is formed:

Consonant addition:

Verb	Abstract Noun
destroy 'to ruin by tearing down'	destruction 'the act of destroying'
apply 'to put on, to put into effect'	application 'the act of applying, the act of using'

The consonant *c*, which is not in the verb *destroy*, appears in the noun *destruction*, and also in the noun *application*.

Table 3

Verb	Abstract Noun
produce 'to make'	production
reduce 'to make less or smaller'	reduction
prescribe 'to order, to require'	prescription
describe 'to tell or write about'	description
perceive 'to be aware through the senses'	perception
receive 'to take, to be given'	reception
apply 'to put on, to put into effect'	application
join 'to bring, put or come together'	junction
destroy 'to ruin by tearing down'	destruction

Exercises: Table 3

8.7 Give the appropriate noun.

	Verb	Noun
Example:	perceive 'to be aware through the senses'	perception

a.   inscribe
'to write on a surface'   _____

b.   transcribe
'to copy in writing or typewriting'   _____

c.   deceive
'to mislead, to use deceit'   _____

d.   subscribe
'to arrange and pay to get a
magazine or a service'   _____

e.   receive
'to take, to be given'   _____

f.   reduce
'to make less or smaller'   _____

g.   absorb
'to take in or suck up a liquid'   _____

h.   imply
'to suggest'   _____

i.   join
'to bring, put or come together'   _____

j.   conceive
'to think up, to imagine'   _____

Unit 8

k.   destroy
        'to ruin by tearing down'   _____

l.   seduce
        'to attract, to lure'   _____

8.8 Create an adjective by adding the suffix *-ive* 'of or having to do with, tending to' to the bound form of the verb.

	<u>Verb</u>	<u>Adjective</u>
Example:	describe	<u>descriptive</u> 'describing, using description'

a.   destroy
                                           _____
                                           'tending to destroy'

b.   prescribe
                                           _____
                                           'that prescribes, established by long use or custom'

c.   deceive
                                           _____
                                           'tending to deceive'

d.   absorb
                                           _____
                                           'able to absorb'

e.   produce
                                           _____
                                           'capable of producing'

f.   perceive
                                           _____
                                           'having the power of perception, insightful'

g.   receive
                                           _____
                                           'able or willing to receive ideas or suggestions'

h.   seduce
                                           _____

Unit 8

'alluring, tending to seduce'

Verbs and Their Abstract Nouns Ending in *-sion* or *-ssion*

A number of verbs take *-sion* or *-ssion* to form their corresponding noun. This pattern is often found with verbs that end in *-de* or *-t*. The *-ion* of these abstract nouns is the suffix you are familiar with, and which means 'act, state, result, condition, or process'.

Verb	Abstract Noun
divide 'to separate into parts'	division 'the act of dividing, the state of being divided'
permit 'to allow, to let'	permission 'the act of permitting, consent'

The second consonant *d* in *divide* corresponds to *s* in *division*, and the *t* in *permit* corresponds to *ss* in *permission*. You will have to memorize which nouns have a single *s* and which have a double *s*.

Table 4

Verb	Abstract Noun
invade 'to enter with force'	invasion
decide 'to settle, to make up one's mind'	decision
divide 'to separate into parts'	division
revert 'to go back, to return'	reversion
permit 'to allow, to let'	permission

Exercises: Table 4

8.9 Fill in the blank with the appropriate noun. All the nouns in this exercise are spelled with a single *s*.

Verb	Noun
Example: decide	decision

a.   subvert 'to ruin, to corrupt'   _____

b.   delude 'to deceive'   _____

c.   provide 'to supply, to take care
      for the future'   _____

d.   suspend 'to hang, to remove or exclude' _____

e.   include 'to contain, to let participate' _____

f.   divert 'to turn aside'   _____

g.   erode 'to wear away'   _____

h.   convert 'to change, to turn'   _____

8.10 Fill in the blank with the appropriate noun. All the nouns in this exercise are spelled with double *s*.

	Verb	Noun
Example:	permit	permission

a.   admit 'to acknowledge, to let in'   _____

b.   proceed 'to move forward'   _____

c.   recede 'to move back, down or away'   _____

d.   commit 'to do (a crime), to involve oneself' _____

e.   transmit 'to pass along, to send signals' _____

f.   emit 'to give off, to express, to send signals'_____

8.11 Create an adjective by adding the suffix *-ive* 'of or having to do with, tending

Unit 8

to' to the appropriate bound form of the verb.

	Verb	Adjective
Example:	divide	<u>divisive</u> 'tending or serving to divide'
a.	invade	_____ 'tending to invade or spread'
b.	explode	_____ 'tending to explode or erupt'
c.	recede	_____ 'tending to go back'
d.	decide	_____ 'settling something beyond question; crucially important'
e.	include	_____ 'including much'
f.	subvert	_____ 'tending or designed to destroy'
g.	evade	_____ 'tending or trying to evade'
h.	permit	_____ 'allowing a great deal of freedom'
i.	exceed	_____ 'going beyond what is right or necessary; too much'

Post-test

Part A Fill in the blank with the appropriate word.

Unit 8   109

Example: describe, description

Please <u>describe</u> what you saw.

Your <u>description</u> of the thief was excellent.

a.   workable, workability

He never took into account the _____ of the project.

John's solution to the problem is _____ .

b.   brilliant, brilliance

The _____ diamond glistened in the sunlight.

The _____ of the sun blinded him.

c.   triangle, triangular

A _____ figure has three sides.

A _____ has three sides.

d.   conceive, conception

Paula's _____ of the project was different from Bob's.

Can you _____ of a different way to make money?

e.   divide, division, divisive

Alcoholism is a _____ problem within society.

Alcoholism can _____ a family.

The family _____ can sometimes be permanent.

f.   permit, permission, permissive

I got my parents' _____ to go to the movies.

My parents _____ me to go to the movies.

_____ parents give their children too much freedom.

Part B Complete the definition of each word.

Example: exclusion 'the act or state of <u>excluding</u>'

a.   juncture ' the state of being _____ed '

b.   applicable 'capable of being _____ed'

c.   destructible 'capable of being _____ed'

d.   applicant 'a person who is _____ing'

e.   excess 'the act or an example of _____ing'

f.   defensible 'capable of _____ed'

Part C Identify the grammatical function (i.e., part of speech) of each word. (**Hint:** use your knowledge of suffixes to help you.)

Example: a <u>workable</u> solution   <u>adjective</u>

a.   They <u>perceive</u> the problem.   _____

b.   a wedding <u>reception</u>   _____

c.   a <u>perceptive</u> student

d.   Did you <u>subscribe</u> to the magazine?   _____

e.   What is your <u>title</u>?   _____

f.   two <u>credible</u> witnesses   _____

g.   a medical <u>prescription</u>   _____

h.   a child with no <u>patience</u>   _____

i.   a <u>subversive</u> political party   _____

j.   <u>muscular</u> pains   _____

k.   an <u>elegant</u> gown   _____

l.   poor <u>visibility</u>   _____

UNIT 9

SOME COMMON BOUND ROOTS

Pretest

1. What is the root of *audible* and what does it mean?

2. What are the two meanings of the root *val* in *valid* and *valor*?

3. Is the root of *terror* the same as *territory*?

4. If fraternal means 'brotherly', what does *fraternity* mean?

In this unit you will learn more about bound roots and their suffixes that form many English words.

Goals:

- One goal is to learn to recognize some common bound roots in English.
- Another goal is to analyze unfamiliar words by recognizing the bound roots and familiar suffixes in the words.

Bound Roots

In Unit 6 you were introduced to bound forms; bound forms cannot stand by themselves but require the presence of a prefix or suffix. Some of the bound forms you have been introduced to are roots: roots form the core of the word. For example, nominee has *nomin* 'name' as its root and -*ee* 'one that is or receives' as its suffix. The suffix modifies the meaning of the root, so nominee means 'one that is named'.

Some of the bound forms you have studied contain a root and a prefix or a suffix. For instance, *evacuee* was analyzed containing the bound form *evacu* 'removed' and suffix -*ee*. However, the bound form *evacu* can be further analyzed as containing a prefix *e-* 'out' and the root *vac* 'empty'. Hence we derive the meaning of 'empty out, remove', so *evacuee* literally means 'one who is removed'.

Unit 9   113

This unit will focus on many common roots that combine with suffixes.

The roots in this unit are listed alphabetically and divided into four tables to make them more accessible.

Roots A-F

Table 1

Form	Meaning	Example
ali, altr	'other, different'	alias 'other name'
ann, enn	'year'	annual 'yearly'
aud	'hear'	audible 'capable of being heard'
cap, capt	'take, hold'	capture 'to take by force, seize'
capit, capt	'head, chief, leader'	capital 'the chief city'
cert	'sure, true'	certify 'to make certain'
corp	'body'	corporal 'of or relating to the body'
cred	'believe'	credible 'believable'
dict	'say, speak'	diction 'the style of speaking or writing'
doc, doct	'teach'	doctrine 'teachings, what is taught'
dur	'hard, strong, lasting'	durable 'capable of lasting'
fac, fact	'do, make'	faculty 'ability to act or do'
fin	'end, complete, limit'	final 'last, at the end'
flor	'flower'	floral 'of or relating to flowers'
flu, fluct	'flow'	fluid 'flowing'
frag, fract	'break'	fracture 'a break; to break'
frater, fratr	'brother'	fraternal 'brotherly'

Exercises: Table 1

9.1 Complete the definition of each word by filling in the blank.

Example: durable   'capable of <u>lasting</u>'

a.   finite   'having _____'

Unit 9

b.   florist   'someone who works with _____'

c.   dictate   'to _____aloud'

d.   credulous   'inclined to _____'

e.   auditory   'of or relating to _____'

f.   captive   'someone _____as prisoner'

9.2 Using the suffix given create the word that corresponds to the definition.

Example: 'capable of lasting' (-able)   <u>durable</u>

a.   'a yearly payment' (-u-ity)   _____

b.   'to flow unsteadily' (-u-ate)   _____

c.   'easily taught' (-ile)   _____

d.   'a broken piece' (-ment)   _____

e.   'a dead body' (-se)   _____

f.   'a brotherhood' (-n-ity)   _____

9.3 Indicate whether the meaning given for each word is true or false.

Example: annual   'yearly'   <u>true</u>

a.   facility   'the quality of being easy to do'_____

b.   audio   'something seen'   _____

c.   altruism   'selfishness'   _____

d.   credit   'belief in the truth of something'_____

e.   certificate   'a document that certifies   _____
                      something'

f.   captain   'a follower'   _____

9.4 Match each word to its synonym (i.e, a word with similar meaning).

<u>Synonyms</u>

Example: finish   <u>complete_____</u>   listeners

a.   floret   _____   complete

b.   fraction   _____   small flower

c.   audience   _____   body of material

d.   duration   _____   foreigner

e.   fluent   _____   a saying

f.   corpus   _____   mathematical fragment

g.   alien   _____   length of time

h.   dictum   _____   flowing

Roots G-M

Table 2

Form	Meaning	Example
gen	'birth, produce, race'	generate 'to produce'
grat	'pleasing, thankful'	grateful 'thankful'

jur, just	'law'	justice 'lawfulness'
leg	'law, read'	legal 'of or relating to the law'
liber	'free'	liberate 'to free'
lit	'letter, read, word'	literate 'able to read and write'
loc	'location, place'	locale 'a place'
magn	'great'	magnify 'to make greater'
mater, matr	'mother'	maternal 'motherly'
medi	'middle'	median 'of or relating to the middle'
migr	'move to new place'	migrate 'to move'
min	'least, smallest'	minimum 'the least amount'
mit, miss	'send'	mission 'a sending or being sent'
mor, mort	'death'	mortal 'of or relating to death'
mot	'move'	motion 'movement'

Exercises: Table 2

9.5 Complete the definition of each word by filling in the blank.

Example: mortal 'of or relating to <u>death</u>'

a. jurist 'one having a thorough knowledge of _____'

b. literacy 'ability to _____'

c. magnate 'a person of _____ wealth'

d. mediate 'holding a _____ position'

e. minute 'very _____'

f. motor 'thing that causes _____'

9.6 Using the suffix given create the word that corresponds to the definition.

Example: 'of or relating to death' (-al) <u>mortal</u>

Unit 9

a. 'the birth of something' (-esis) _____

b. 'capable of being read' (-ible) _____

c. 'moving from one place to another' (-ant) _____

d. 'motherhood' (-n-ity) _____

e. 'establish in a place' (-ate) _____

f. 'the state of being grateful' (-itude) _____

9.7 Indicate whether the meaning given for each word is true or false.

Example: mortal   'relating to birth'   <u>false</u>

a. genus   'a biological classification'   _____

b. jury   'people who decide in a law case'   _____

c. minuscule   'extremely large'   _____

d. medial   'of or relating to the side'   _____

e. missionary 'someone sent on a mission'   _____

f. liberal 'open minded'   _____

9.8 Match each word to its synonym (i.e., a word with similar meaning).

<u>Synonym</u>

Example: legitimate   <u>lawful_____</u>   freedom

a. missile   _____   purpose

b. moribund   _____   dignified woman

Unit 9   118

c.	gratuity	_____	not worldwide
d.	mortician	_____	lawful
e.	liberty	_____	rocket
f.	motive	_____	tip
g.	local	_____	undertaker
h.	matron	_____	dying

Roots N-R

Table 3

Form	Meaning	Example
nat	'born, birth'	natal 'of or relating to birth'
nav	'boat, ship'	navy 'ships of war'
numer	'number'	numerous 'many in number'
oper, opus	'work'	operate 'to work'
pac	'peace'	pacify 'to make peaceful'
pat, pass	'suffer, experience, feel'	patient 'someone who suffers'
pater, patr	'father'	paternal 'fatherly'
pen	'penalty, wrong'	penal 'of or relating to punishment'
pend	'hang, heavy'	pendant 'something that hangs'
plen	'full'	plenty 'a full supply; enough'
popul	'people'	populate 'to people'
pot	'power, ability'	potent 'powerful'
prim	'first'	primal 'first, chief'
punct	'point, prick, pierce'	puncture 'to pierce; a piercing'
reg, rect	'rule, right, straight'	rectify 'to make right'
rot	'round, turn'	rotund 'round'

Exercises: Table 3

Unit 9

9.9 Complete the definition of each word by filling in the blank.

Example: rectify   'to make <u>right</u>'
a.   populous   'full of_____'

b.   numerical   'relating to_____'

c.   passion   'very strong_____ing'

d.   penitent   'sorrow for doing_____'

e.   operable   'fit or able to be_____'

f.   native   'belonging to by_____'

9.10 Using the suffix given create the word that corresponds to the definition.

Example: 'to make right' (-ify)   <u>rectify</u>

a.   'to steer a ship ' (-ig-ate)   _____

b.   'hanging down' (-ul-ous)   _____

c.   'full' (-ary)   _____

d.   'fatherhood' (-n-ity)   _____

e.   'having parts that turn' (-ary)   _____

f.   'to place a point at the end of a sentence'
      (-u-ate)   _____

9.11 Indicate whether the meaning given for each word is true or false.

Example: pacific   'peaceful'   <u>true</u>

a.   rectitude   'moral uprightness'   _____

Unit 9
                                                                    120

b. primary 'last in order' _____

c. nativity 'relating to one's death' _____

d. potentate 'powerful ruler' _____

e. patience 'ability to accept things calmly' _____

f. rotor 'machine part that does not turn' _____

9.12 Match each word to its synonym (a word with similar meaning).

Synonym

Example: pacific <u>calm_____</u> punish

a. populace _____ hanging

b. numerate _____ power

c. penalize _____ calm

d. rotunda _____ people

e. pendent _____ inactive

f. potency _____ straight intestine

g. passive _____ circular building

h. rectum _____ count

Unit 9

Roots S-V

Table 4

Form	Meaning	Example
sanct	'holy'	sanctify 'to make holy'
sent, sens	'feel, aware'	sentiment 'feeling'
simil, simul	'similar, resemble'	similar 'similar'
techn	'skill, ability'	technique 'a skill'
term	'end, boundary, limit'	terminate 'to end'
terr	'earth, land'	territory 'an area of land'
test	'witness'	testimony 'statement from a witness'
tut, tuit	'teach'	tutor 'a private teacher'
vac	'empty'	vacuum 'emptiness'
val	'value, worth, brave'	valid 'having value'
var	'change, different'	variable 'changeable'
ver	'true, truth'	verify 'to prove to be true'
vis	'see'	vision 'seeing'
vit, viv	'life, alive, lively'	vital 'of or relating to life'

Exercises: Table 4

9.13 Complete the definition of each word by filling in the blank.

Example: terminate 'to <u>end</u>'

a. sensory 'relating to the _____'

b. technician 'one who has _____ in the mechanical arts'

c. vacate 'to leave _____'

d. simulate 'to _____'

Unit 9

e.   verity   'the state of being _____'

f.   sanctuary   'a _____ place'

9.14 Using the suffix given create the word that corresponds to the definition.

Example: 'to end' (-ate)   <u>terminate</u>

a.   'that can be seen' (-u-al)   _____

b.   'full of life' (-id)   _____

c.   'a geographical area' (-ain)   _____

d.   'great courage' (-our)   _____

e.   'differing' (-ious)   _____

f.   'a finishing point' (-inus)   _____

9.15 Indicate whether the meaning given for each word is true or false.

Example: vacuum   'fullness'   <u>false</u>

a.   similitude   'resemblance'   _____

b.   testament   'a solemn agreement'   _____

c.   variety   'sameness'   _____

d.   tuition   'payment for instruction'   _____

e.   sanctity   'quality of being unholy'   _____

f.   terrestrial   'of the earth, of the land'   _____

9.16 Match each word to its synonym (i.e., a word with similar meaning).

Unit 9   123

Example: termination _end_____   difference

a.   similitude   _____   instruction

b.   sentient   _____   empty

c.   variety   _____   worth

d.   tutelage   _____   resemblance

e.   vivacious   _____   aware

f.   visit   _____   end

g.   value   _____   go to see

h.   vacuous   _____   lively

Post-test

Part A Choose the correct definition.

Example: vacant   _____ 'full'
                          ___✓___ 'empty'

a.   valiant   _____ 'courageous'
                    _____ 'fearful'

b.   testate   _____ 'having an invalid will'
                    _____ 'having a valid will'

c.   alienate   _____ 'to become hostile to others'
                    _____ 'to become friendly with others'

d.   fraternize   _____ 'to be unfriendly'
                    _____ 'to be friendly'

Unit 9   124

e. literal   _____ 'relating to the exact letter'
                       _____ 'imaginative'

f. primitive   _____ 'cultured'
                       _____ 'from the earliest times'

g. pacifism   _____ 'opposition to war'
                       _____ 'support of war'

h. penalty   _____ 'punishment'
                       _____ 'reward'

i. navigable   _____ 'that ships cannot travel on'
                       _____ 'that ships can travel on'

j. sensuous   _____ 'of or relating to the mind'
                       _____ 'of or relating to the senses'

Part B Fill in the blank with the appropriate word.

Example: floral, florist

The floral arrangement looked very beautiful.

The florist in the mall sells beautiful flowers.

a. audible, audition

The actor was told that he got the leading role in the play right after his

_____.

His voice was barely _____ because there was so much
noise coming from the street.

b. liberate, liberty

The prime minister said he would _____ all the political

Unit 9   125

prisoners currently in jail.

A democratic government must protect the _____ of its citizens.

c.   naval, navy

The _____ commander met with the press after the accident aboard the ship.

Canada has a small _____.

d.   terminus, terminates

The railway _____ in Prince George.

Its _____ is in Prince George.

e.   populate, popular

The Rolling Stones are still one of the most _____ rock bands in the world.

Most of the people who _____ this area are from the province of Quebec.

UNIT 10

PREFIXES AND ROOTS

Pretest

1. What is the prefix in *emit* and what does it mean?

2. What are the two meanings of the prefix *–in* as in *inflammable* and *inscription*?

3. What are the variant forms of *dis-* and *com-*?

4. Does the same root appear in *ascend* and in *descend*?

In this unit you will learn more about the prefixes of English, and how they combine with roots to form English words.

Goals:

- One goal is to learn more about the prefixes of English.
- Another goal is to understand unfamiliar words by recognizing the prefixes and the roots occurring in them.
- A third goal is to learn more about common prefixes that appear in several different forms, and which are often attached to bound roots.

Variant Forms of Prefixes

In Unit 2 you learned that the prefixes *in-* 'not' and *en-* 'to put into or onto, to make' both had variant forms. The shape of the prefix changed depending on the word to which it was attached. Here you will learn about other prefixes that have variant forms. Once again, the form of the prefix will depend on the word or root to which the prefix is attached. For instance, *dis-* 'apart, away' has a variant form *di-*:

    dis-: disrupt 'to break apart'   di-: divert 'to turn away'

It is important for you vocabulary development to be able to recognize a prefix and its variant forms.

Some of the prefixes that are listed below have been introduced to you in Units 1 and 2, and others will be new to you. Some prefixes that you were introduced to in earlier units have particular meanings when they occur with bound roots: as you know, ex- in ex-wife means 'former', but in exhale 'to breathe out' it means 'out'. It also occurs with a slightly different for in emit 'to send out, to give off'. The purpose of this unit is to teach you the common prefixes that combine with roots as well as independent words, their meanings, and the variant forms of those prefixes that have more than one shape.

Table 1

Forms	Meaning	Example
ab-, a-	'away, from, off'	abduct 'to lead away' avert 'to turn away'
ad-, at-, as-, ap-, af-, ac-, ag-, ar-, al-, an-, ab-, a-	'to, toward'	adhere 'to stick to' attract 'to draw to oneself' approve 'to consent to'
com-, con-, col-, cor-, co-	'with, together, completely'	compel 'to force completely' collect 'to gather together'
de-	'remove, away, off, down'	dehydrate 'to remove water from'
dis-, di-	'apart, away, aside'	disrupt 'to break apart' divert 'to turn aside'
ex-, e-	'out, from, thoroughly'	exhale 'to breathe out' emit 'to send out, to give off'
in-, im-, il-, ir-	'in, into, on, upon, very'	inscription 'words written on' inflammable 'very flammable'
per-	'through, thoroughly'	percolate 'to pass through'

Unit 10

pre-	'before, beforehand'	precede 'to go before'
pro-	'forward, forth, out'	progress 'to move forward'
re-	'back, again'	retain 'to hold back'
sub-	'below, under'	submerge 'to put under water'
trans-, tran-	'across, over, beyond'	transmit 'to send over, pass on' transcend 'to go beyond'

Exercises: Table 1

10.1 Complete the definition for each word by filling in the blank with the meaning of the prefix.

Example: exhale   <u>'to breathe out'</u>

a.   inhale   'to breathe _____'

b.   rehydrate   'to put water _____"

c.   cohesive (as people in a group)   'a sticking _____'

d.   descend (stairs)   'to go _____'

e.   recur   'to happen _____'

f.   proceed   'to move _____'

g.   regain   'to get _____'

h.   assimilate   'to become similar _____"

i.   annihilate   'to reduce _____ nothing, to destroy completely'

j.   predict   'to tell _____, to forecast'

10.2 Using the root provided and choosing the appropriate prefix, create the word that matches the definition.

Example: cede 'go'

        'to go back'   <u>recede</u>

        'to go before'   <u>precede</u>

a. flect 'bend'

        'to bend back'   _____

        'to bend away'   _____

b. ject 'throw'

        'to throw out'   _____

        'to throw back'   _____

        'to throw forward'   _____

c. migr 'move'

        'to move into a country' _____

        'to move out of a country' _____

d. mit 'send'

        'to let go through, allow' _____

        'to send over'   _____

        'to send out'   _____

'to send money back in payment'   _____

e. duct 'lead'

       'to bring in, introduce'   _____

       'to carry off, take away by force'   _____

       'to make an orchestra work together'   _____

       'to take away (down), subtract'   _____

10.3 Indicate whether the meaning given for each word is true or false, based on your knowledge of prefixes.

Example: <u>ex</u>hale   'to breathe <u>in</u>'   <u>false</u>

a.   <u>col</u>lapse   ' to fold or push <u>together</u>'   _____

b.   <u>im</u>merse   'to plunge <u>out</u>'   _____

c.   <u>ab</u>hor   'to shrink <u>away</u> from in horror'   _____

d.   <u>con</u>cur   'to run <u>together</u>, to agree'   _____

e.   <u>ad</u>hesive   'falling <u>apart</u>'   _____

f.   <u>dis</u>miss   'to send <u>in</u>'   _____

10.4 Complete each sentence by filling in the blank with the correct word from the list provided to you.

List 1: cede (ceed) 'go'   preceded, recede, concede

Example: We will <u>concede</u> that you are right when you provide the statistics to prove it.

a.   The invention of the motor car _____ the invention of the airplane.

b.   The hairline of most men begins to _____ in their forties, and some men eventually become bald.

List 2: tract 'pull, draw' detracts, attracts, protract

a.   The sweetness of honey _____ the bears.

b.   The Wilsons decided to _____ their vacation by an extra two weeks.

c.   That ugly picture frame _____ from the painting.

List 3: lapse 'fall'   elapsed, collapsed, relapsed

a.   That old bridge _____ because it was never repaired.

b.   A long time _____ before a new bridge was built.

c.   The husband and wife spoke for a few moments then _____ into silence.

10.5 Complete the definition for each word by fill in the blank with the meaning of the prefix.

Example: repel   'to push <u>back</u>'

a.   extend   'to stretch _____'

Unit 10

b.   erupt   'to break _____'

c.   export   'to send goods _____ 'of one's country'

d.   assign   'to appoint _____ 'a post'

e.   invoke   'to call _____ 'in prayer'

f.   ingest   'to take _____ 'the body for digestion'

g.   pervert   'to turn _____ 'away from the normal'

h.   provocative   'tending to call _____ 'thought, anger, action'

10.6 Using the root provided and choosing the appropriate prefix, create the word that matches the definition.
Example: cede 'go'

                'to go back'   <u>recede</u>
                'to go before'   <u>precede</u>

a.   rupt 'break'

                'to break out'   _____

                'to break apart'   _____

                'to thoroughly break one's
                honesty, to make dishonest'   _____

b.   pel 'drive, push'

                'to push forward'   _____

                'to drive away, scatter'   _____

                'to drive out'   _____

Unit 10   133

'to drive back' _____

c.   vert 'turn'

       'to turn back' _____

       'to turn away, avoid' _____

       'to turn aside, deviate' _____

d.   verge 'turn, bend'

       'to turn away from a point' _____

       'to meet together in a point' _____

e.   port 'carry, send (goods)'

       'to send goods
into a country' _____

       'to send goods
out of a country' _____

f.   press 'press, squeeze'

       'to press back, to keep down' _____

       'to press down, to make sad' _____

       'to squeeze together' _____

10.7 Indicate whether the meaning given for each word is true or false, based on your knowledge of prefixes.

Example: inflammable 'very flammable'   <u>true</u>

a.   <u>re</u>voke   'to call <u>out</u>'   _____

b.   <u>di</u>stend   'to stretch <u>apart</u>, stretch <u>out</u>'   _____

c.   <u>de</u>tain   'to hold <u>down</u>, delay'   _____

d.   <u>dis</u>solve   'to loosen <u>beforehand</u>'   _____

e.   <u>ab</u>solve   'to declare free <u>from</u> blame'   _____

f.   <u>al</u>lude   'to refer <u>with</u>'   _____

10.8 Complete each sentence by filling in the blank with the correct word from the list provided to you.

List 1: puls 'drive, push'   compulsion, expulsion, propulsion, repulsive

Example: The girl found the boy's bad breath <u>repulsive</u>.

a.   I have such a _____ to buy a new dress for the party.

b.   Cheating on assignments will result in your _____ from college.

c.   The plane's new jet engine has better _____ than the old engine.

List 2: gress 'step, move'   progress, regressed, ingress, digress

a.   To _____ is to move away from the main topic in talking or writing.

Unit 10   135

b. As she aged, her mind _____ further into the past.

c. The girl's _____ in school was held up by her long illness last year.

d. A high fence prevented _____ to the soccer field.

List 3: struct 'build'   instructions, destruction, construction

a. The earthquake caused a lot of _____ in the village.

b. After the damaged houses were torn down, the _____ of new houses began.

c. The villagers followed _____ on how to build safer houses.

List 4: voke, voc 'call'   revoked, evokes, invoked, advocate

a. The priest _____ the help of a god after the earthquake.

b. Your driver's license will be _____ if you are caught driving while you are drunk.

c. A good joke _____ a laugh.

d. Susan chose a well-known criminal lawyer as her_____.

Post-test

Part A Find the correct word to match the definition.

revoke	inhale	succeed
project	converge	proceed
erupt	detract	invert
describe	perceive	

Example: 'to break out'   <u>erupt</u>

a.   'to throw forward'   _____

b.   'to write down words'   _____

c.   'to breathe in'   _____

d.   'to go forward'   _____

e.   'to come next after'   _____

f.   'to call back'   _____

g.   'to turn in, turn upside down'   _____

h.   'be aware of through the senses' _____

i.   'to meet together in a point'   _____

j.   'to take away from'   _____

Part B Choose the synonym for each word.

Example: immigrate: move in, move out' <u>move in</u>

a.   absent 'be away, be in'   _____

b.   inspect: look into, look away from   _____

c.   ascend: climb up, climb down   _____

d.   expel: drive back, drive out   _____

e.   deport: send away, send forward   _____

f.   transport: carry to another place, carry out _____

g.   explode: burst in, burst out   _____

Unit 10   137

h.   invest: put money in, take money out   _____

i.   dissect: cut apart, cut thoroughly   _____

UNIT 11

COMPOUND WORDS

Pretest

      1. What is a compound word?

      2. How many types of compound words does English have?

      3. Does *catfish* mean 'a cat resembling a fish' or 'a fish representing a cat'?

      4.What are the two roots joined together in *astronaut*, and what does each mean?

      5. What is the most appropriate meaning of *arch* in *archbishop* and *arch* in *matriarch*?

In this unit you will learn what a compound word is, and you will learn about the two types of compounds that are commonly found in English.

Goals:

- One goal is learn what a compound word is.
- Another goal is to analyze unfamiliar words by recognizing their compound structure.
- A third goal is to recognize some common bound roots that occur in compound words.

Compounds Containing Two Words

English has many compound words which were formed by joining two independent words together. For instance, *homework* was formed by putting *home* and *work* together. The meaning of the compound word is determined by the meaning of each of its components; thus *homework* refers to work that is done at home.

Unit 11

Compound words of this type have a particular structure. Knowing this structure will help you to determine the meaning of the compound word accurately. The structure includes a general term and a specific term. The second part of a compound word is usually the general term, like *work* in *homework*. The first part is much more specific and modifies the meaning of the more general term. So *home* in *homework* specifies work that is done in the home and not elsewhere. Many English compound words follow this pattern.

Table 1

Example	Modifier + General Term	Meaning
doorstep	door + step	'a step at a door'
housemaid	house + maid	'a maid who cleans a house'
horseman	horse + man	'a man on a horse'
workplace	work + place	'one's place of work'

The meaning of some compound words may not be as literal as the examples above. *Hothouse* refers to a building that is made hot for the specific purpose of growing plants, and means the same as *greenhouse*. Similarly *green* in *greenhouse* refers to the growing of plants.

Exercises: Table 1

11.1 Underline the correct form of the compound word from the two choices given to you.

Example: a man on a horse: manhorse   <u>horseman</u>

a.   a bird that lives by the sea   seabird   birdsea

b.   a bell near the front door   doorbell   belldoor

c.   a ship used for war   shipwar   warship

d.   a shoe for a horse   horseshoe   shoehorse

e.   the top of a house   tophouse   housetop

Unit 11

f.	work done on or with paper	workpaper	paperwork
g.	work involving books	bookwork	workbook
h.	a book used for work	bookwork	workbook

11.2 Create the appropriate compound word corresponding to the following phrases.

Example: work done at home   <u>homework</u>

a.	a knob on a door	_____
b.	a friend who is a boy	_____
c.	a bench for work	_____
d.	a maker of paper	_____
e.	a sled pulled by dogs	_____
f.	a house for a dog	_____
g.	a man at the door (who opens and closes it)	_____
h.	the shore of the sea	_____
i.	the shore of the lake	_____
j.	the bank of the river	_____

11.3 Create a compound word matching the definition given and using the suggested components.

Example: one's amount (load) of work   <u>workload</u>

a.   one who guards (keeper) a door   _____

b.   a woman (wife) who stays at home (house)   _____

c.   a person (head) with a bad temper (hot)   _____

d.   a creature somewhat resembling
a horse (horse) and living in the sea   _____

e.   a fish that looks and acts as fierce as a wolf   _____

f.   a type of dog (hound) once used
to hunt wolves (wolf)   _____

g.   a fierce fight (fight) between dogs; a fierce
fight between warplanes   _____

h.   in disfavor with somebody, like a dog (dog)
alone in its house   <u>(in the)</u>_____

Compounds Containing Latin and Greek Roots

A different type of English compound contains Latin or Greek roots joined together. Often the roots are bound, that is, they do not occur by themselves as independent English words. This type of compound is common, but it is often more difficult to analyze because of the bound roots. Some examples of this type of compound are *geography* and *agriculture*.

geography: geo 'earth' + graphy 'science'
'the science of the earth'

agriculture: agri 'field' + culture 'cultivation'
'the cultivation of the fields, farming'

Unit 11   142

There are some very common Latin and Greek roots that occur in a number of English compounds. It is worthwhile to remember their meanings to help you remember the meaning of the whole word, and to help you determine the meaning of an unfamiliar word.

Table 2

Form	Meaning	Example
arch-	chief, principal	archbishop 'principal bishop'
-arch	ruler	matriarch 'a mother and ruler of a tribe or family'
-archy	rule, government	matriarchy 'rule by a mother'
astro-	star, outer space	astronomy 'science of the stars'
-cide	kill	germicide 'substance that kills germs'
geo-	earth, ground	geography 'science of the earth'
-graph	draw, write, picture, record	seismograph 'instrument for recording earthquakes'
-graphy	science, writing, describing	geography 'science of the earth'
hydro-	water, hydrogen	hydrotherapy 'therapy using water'
-logy	study, doctrine, science, discussion	biology 'science of life'
matri-	mother	matriarch 'a mother and ruler of a tribe or family'
-meter	measure	speedometer 'a device for measuring speed'
-naut	sailor, traveler	astronaut 'a space traveler'
-nomy	arrangement, science, management	astronomy 'the science of the stars'
-path	person suffering, medical practitioner	psychopath 'person suffering a severe disorder of the mind'
patri-	father	patriarch 'a father and ruler of a tribe or family'
-phile	lover, loving	Francophile 'a lover of French culture'
-philia	tendency, unnatural attraction	pedophilia 'unnatural sexual attraction to children'
-phobia	fear, hatred	claustrophobia 'fear of enclosed

		places'
-phone increasing	sound, speak	microphone 'instrument for
		the loudness of sounds'
psycho-	mind	psychoanalysis 'analysis and treatment of the mind'
-scope	see, observe	microscope 'instrument for observing mall things'
uni-	one	uniform 'all alike, unchanging'

The hyphen attached to the beginning or end of each root shows where the root is joined to another root. Some roots form the first part of a compound; others form the second part. Some roots can occur in both positions, but sometimes there is a slight difference in meaning, as with *arch*.

Exercises: Table 2

11.4 Make compound words to match each definition, using *-cide* 'kill' as the second root of the compound.

geno- 'race of people'   patri- 'father'   infanti- 'infant, child'
herbi 'plant'   insecti- 'insect'   spermi- 'sperm'
sui- 'self'   homi- 'human being'

Example: 'the murder of an infant or young child'   <u>infanticide</u>

a.   'substance that kills plants'   _____

b.   'the killing of one's father'   _____

c.   'the killing of oneself'   _____

d.   'the murder of a human being'   _____

e.   'substance that kills sperm'   _____

f.   'substance that kills insects'   _____

g.   'the killing of a race of people'   _____

Unit 11

144

11.5 Make compound words to match each definition, using -*logy* 'theory, doctrine, science, discussion' as the second root of the compound.

socio- 'society'   anthropo- 'mankind'   radio- 'radiation'
astro- 'star'   theo- 'god'   zoo- 'animal life'
phraseo- 'words'   grapho- 'writing'   patho- 'disease'

Example: 'the science of society'   <u>sociology</u>

a.   'the style of wording or verbal expression'   _____

b.   'the science of mankind'   _____

c.   'the study of the nature of God'   _____

d.   'the study of handwriting'   _____

e.   'the science of animal life'   _____

f.   'the study of diseases'   _____

g.   'the branch of medicine using radiation'   _____

h.   'the doctrine of the influence of stars
      on events'   _____

11.6 Make a compound using -*phobia* 'fear, hatred' as the second root of the compound.

agora- 'public place'   arachno- 'spiders'
xeno- 'foreigner'   acro- 'height'
claustro 'enclosed place'   homo- 'homosexual'

Example: 'a fear of heights'   <u>acrophobia</u>

a.   'a fear of public places and open spaces'   _____

Unit 11   145

b.   'an aversion to homosexual people
      and practices'   _____

c.   'a hatred or fear of foreigners
      or foreign things   _____

d.   'a fear of spiders'   _____

e.   'a fear of enclosed places'   _____

11.7 Make a compound word by joining the appropriate roots. Any new roots not provided in **Table 2** are given to you in parenthesis.

Example: 'a <u>speaker</u> of <u>English</u>' (anglo-)   <u>Anglophone</u>

a.   'a device for <u>measuring</u> <u>water</u>'   _____

b.   'a <u>lover</u> of <u>books</u>' (biblio-)   _____

c.   'a device for transmitting <u>sound</u>
      over a <u>distance</u>' (tele-)   _____

d.   'the <u>science</u> of <u>environment</u>' (eco-)   _____

e.   'a <u>picture</u> made by using <u>light</u> (photo-)
      on a film'   _____

f.   'an instrument for <u>observing</u> over
      a <u>distance</u>' (tele-)   _____

g.   'a device for <u>measuring</u> <u>heat</u>' (thermo-) _____

h.   '<u>science</u> of the <u>mind</u>'   _____

i.   '<u>rule</u> by <u>oneself</u> (mon-)'   _____

j.   'vehicle with <u>one</u> <u>wheel</u> (-cycle)'   _____

11.8 Fill in the blank with the appropriate meaning.

Example: astrophysics   'the science of the physical properties of the <u>stars</u>'

a.   archangel   'the _____ angel'

b.   cosmonaut   'a _____ in space, an astronaut'

c.   autonomy   'self _____, independence'

d.   gastronomy   'the art or _____ of good eating'

e.   unicorn   'a mythical animal with _____ horn'

f.   megaphone   'a device that increases _____'

g.   francophone   'a person who _____ French'

h.   necrophilia   'an _____ for the dead'

i.   hemophilia   'a _____ to bleed'

j.   Sinology   'the _____ of the Chinese'

Post-test

Part A Which word of each pair is a compound word? You can recognize a compound word by its two roots.

Example: aeronaut 'a pilot or traveler in an airship'
           nautical 'of or relating to seamen, navigation, or ships'

                    <u>aeronaut</u>

a.   graphic 'formed by writing or drawing'
     phonograph 'an instrument for reproducing sounds on a disc'

_____

b.   stethoscope 'an instrument used to hear the lungs and heart'
scope 'the extent of one's view, the area over which an activity extends'

_____

c.   sexual 'of or relating to sex or the sexes'
unisex 'of or having to do with one style (clothing, haircuts) intended for both sexes'

_____

d.   metrical 'of, relating to or used in measurement'
chronometer 'a clock that measures time very accurately'

_____

e.   psychic 'of the soul or mind, mental, supernatural'
psychosomatic 'of or relating to both mind and body'

Part B Make up two compound words using _boat_ and _house_ to match each definition.

a.   'a house or shelter for boats'   _____

b.   'a boat that can be lived in like a house'   _____

Part C Underline the compound words that you recognize in the following texts.

a. A Canadian judge will begin a crash course in musicology on Monday when he begins hearing evidence in a court case. A man claims he co-wrote several songs with a famous singer and songwriter, but was not given any credits for them.

b. An iceberg is a large mass of ice in the sea that has originated on land. Many result from the breaking off of ice from glaciers. In the north icebergs originate chiefly from Greenland; in the south most break off from Antarctica, an icy land mass covering 14,300,000 square kilometers.

Unit 11

c. North American birds live in a variety of habitats. Seagulls and sandpipers live close to water. Meadowlarks like fields and meadows, whereas blackbirds like marshes and fields. Jays and robins prefer forests.

ANSWER KEY

UNIT 1

1.1
a. pay in advance
b. behave badly
c. visit again
d. not friendly
e. fellow worker
f. former president
g. warn beforehand
h. opposed to democracy
i. superior woman
j. remove frost
k. favoring abortion

1.2
a. Jack is the <u>ex-husband</u> of my friend Mary.
b. My neighbor is <u>anti-union</u>.
c. It is <u>unwise</u> to spend all your money on clothes.
d. A <u>pro-logging</u> party was elected.
e. That child <u>misunderstood</u> me.
f. The campers <u>precut</u> the wood for their fire.
g. Workers <u>de-iced</u> the airplanes wings.
h. Susan and Brian are the <u>co-editors</u> of this newspaper.
i. Mary claims that she can <u>foretell</u> the future of her friends and relatives.
j. The government has built a <u>superhighway</u> on Vancouver Island.

1.3
a. The man is <u>dishonorable</u>.
b. The girl who was <u>unhappy</u> cried for an hour.
c. The boy is a <u>nonsmoker</u>.
d. Those comments were <u>unnecessary</u>.
e. My mother was <u>displeased</u> about my grades.
f. Milk is <u>nonacidic</u>.

1.4
a. re + used   'used again'
b. mis + pronunciation 'wrong pronunciation'
c. dis + like   'not like'

d.	un + sure	'not sure'
e.	non + stick	'not stick'
f.	de + salt	'remove salt from'
g.	non + re + usable	'not usable again'

1.5
a. predawn
b. return
c. co-manage
d. subconscious
e. semi-cooked
f. unfold
g. disconnect

1.6
a. 'half'
b. 'partly'
c. 'in advance'
d. 'before'
e. 'below'
f. 'secondary'
g. 'not'
h. 'do the opposite of'
i. 'fellow'
j. 'together'
k. 'did the opposite of'
l. 'not'

1.7
a. submarine
b. subaquatic
c. semiannual
d. semiliterate
e. semiarid
f. relocate
g. recoil
h. rebound
i. premarital
j. preliterate

1.8

a.   John dislikes <u>anti-Canadian</u> feelings.

b.   John dislikes <u>anti-Cuban policies</u>.

c.   Mary is <u>pro-French</u>.

d.   Mary likes John's <u>pro-Japanese views</u>.

e.   Mary likes <u>pro-technology companies</u>.

Post-test

a.   ex-boyfriend

b.   semicircle

c.   redo

d.   undo

e.   subterranean

f.   reapply

g.   misplayed

h.   defrost

i.   co-exist

j.   predate

k.   disclose

UNIT 2

2.1

a.   impure

b.   illogical

c.   insecure

d.   irrationally

e.   inability

f.   imbalance

g.   irresponsibility

h.   immortal

i.   informal

j.   illegible

2.2

a.   Throwing paper airplanes is <u>not proper</u> behavior during an exam.
(Throwing paper airplanes <u>isn't proper</u> behavior during an exam.)

b.   They <u>did not hold</u> the meeting at a <u>convenient</u> time.
(They <u>didn't hold</u> the meeting at a <u>convenient</u> time.)

c.   At lunch Susan was <u>not polite</u> to my best friend.

(At lunch Susan <u>wasn't polite</u> to my best friend.)
d.   Mary's reply was <u>not relevant</u> to the teacher's question.
       (Mary's reply, <u>wasn't relevant</u> to the teacher's question.)
e.   He <u>did not</u> behave <u>sanely</u> at the dance.
       (He <u>didn't</u> behave <u>sanely</u> at the dance.)
f.   James <u>did not</u> attend classes <u>regularly</u>.
       (James <u>didn't</u> attend classes <u>regularly</u>.)

2.3
a.   endanger
b.   embody
c.   enrage
d.   enlarge
e.   empurple
f.   enforce
g.   empower
h.   ennoble

2.4
a.   enlarged
b.   embedded
c.   enlivened
d.   ensure
e.   enrich
f.   emplaced
g.   entrust

2.6
a.   ant-
b.   anti- 'opposed to'
c.   opposite of
d.   In this case, the *i* in *anti* is lost before the vowel *a* in *arctic*. Another
       example of this is *antacid* (*anti* + *acid*). However, the vowel is not lost in
       anti-aircraft or *anti-American*.

Post-test

Part A
a.   irreparable
b.   incomplete
c.   insignificant

Answer Key

d.   irrelevant
e.   immeasurable
f.   immodest
g.   illegitimate
h.   immobile
i.   illicit
j.   irreverent

Part B

a.   Human activities <u>put</u> animals <u>into danger</u> all over the world.
b.   The company <u>made</u> its operation <u>bigger</u> by 20 percent.
c.   Sally was <u>put into a rage</u> when her basketball team lost the game.
d.   Canadian culture has been <u>improved</u> by immigrants.
e.   The goal of feminism is to <u>provide</u> women <u>with power</u>.

Unit 3

3.1

a.   geologist
b.   reader
c.   oldster
d.   violinist
e.   sweetie
f.   gamester
g.   Italian
h.   girlie
i.   journalist
j.   potter
k.   absentee
l.   comedian

3.2

a.   'one that motors' (drives)
b.   'a native of Europe'
c.   'one that makes gloves'
d.   'a native of Brooklyn'
e.   'one that sails'
f.   'a native of Vietnam'
g.   'one that counsels'
h.   'one that makes puns'
i.   'a person that escapes'

j.   'one that works with electricity'

3.3
a.   John will <u>act</u> in Hamlet.
        John is an <u>actor</u> in a Shakespearean play.
b.   A <u>singer</u> must have voice training if he or she wants to succeed.
        Pavarotti <u>sings</u> opera music.
c.   I want to <u>cycle</u> around the island.
        The <u>cyclist</u> went around the island.
d.   Fred and Amy <u>golfed</u> 18 holes every day of their holiday.
        Fred and Amy are enthusiastic <u>golfers</u>.
e.   The <u>employees</u> listened very carefully to their supervisor.
        The company will <u>employ</u> ten more workers.

3.4
a.   childhood
b.   computer
c.   Catholicism
d.   doggie
e.   stardom
f.   cooker
g.   liberalism
h.   kingdom
i.   sportsmanship
j.   bakery

3.5
a.   'the skill of a workman'
b.   'the period of being a child'
c.   'the doctrine of Darwin'
d.   'the status of a movie star'
e.   'thing that prints'
f.   'a place for nuns'

3.6
a.   distribution
b.   embodiment
c.   defiance
d.   computation
e.   confusion
f.   friendliness

3.7

a.　martyrdom
b.　brotherhood
c.　management
d.　skiing
e.　rigidity
f.　sadness
g.　robbery
h.　growth
i.　fellowship
j.　construction
k.　coverage
l.　cruelty

3.8

a.　strength
b.　length
c.　filth
d.　death
e.　breadth
f.　health

3.9

a.　Margaret is a good person.
　　People notice her goodness.
b.　Margaret is a sad person.
　　People notice her sadness.
c.　Margaret is a friendly person.
　　People notice her friendliness.

3.10

a.　Diamonds are hard.
　　The hardness of diamonds is well known.
b.　Frank and Betty bore me.
　　Bill spent a long day of boredom at the office.
c.　Bob and Sheila are having an argument.
　　They argue all the time.
d.　We eat supper at 6 PM.
　　Their eating of supper was interrupted by a visitor.
e.　My parents will attend the meeting with the principal.

Their <u>attendance</u> at the meeting was noticed.

f. The <u>formation</u> of the Hawaiian islands was due to volcanoes.
Volcanoes can <u>form</u> mountains.

g. We will <u>ship</u> the goods to you on Friday.
The <u>shipment</u> will arrive in the afternoon.

h. The motto of *X-Files* is 'The <u>truth</u> is out there.'
My sister is a <u>true</u> friend.

i. The <u>confusion</u> was great after the robbery.
This problem will <u>confuse</u> you.

j. Vinegar has an <u>acid</u> taste.
The <u>acidity</u> of this wine is overpowering.

k. The <u>spoilage</u> of the food for the picnic was due to the very hot weather.
Food will <u>spoil</u> quickly in hot weather.

l. The soldier received a medal for his <u>bravery</u>.
<u>Brave</u> soldiers receive medals.

Post-test

Part A
a. 'the state of being a hero'
b. 'the skill of a craftsman'
c. 'one that specializes in archeology'
d. 'one that does tricks'
e. 'a dear little doll'

Part B
a. Some athletes can endure a lot of pain. The <u>endurance</u> of Olympic athletes is well-known. However <u>sportsmanship</u> among amateur athletes is better than among Olympic athletes.
b. Volcanoes can erupt without much <u>warning</u>. Their <u>eruptions</u> cause <u>devastation</u>, <u>hardship</u> and <u>disruption</u> for people living near them.
c. My older brother dissolved his <u>partnership</u> in the company; he left to join the <u>priesthood</u>. My younger brother is studying <u>dentistry</u>.

Part C
a. deforestation: prefix   <u>de- 'remove'</u>
                   base word   <u>forest</u>
                   suffix   <u>-ation 'act, process'</u>

'the act or process of clearing of trees'

Answer Key

b. encirclement: prefix   <u>en- 'cause to be, put into'</u>
                    base word   <u>circle</u>
                    suffix   <u>-ment 'act, state'</u>

'the act or state of forming a circle around'

c. inaction: prefix   <u>in- 'not'</u>
                    base word   <u>act</u>
                    suffix   <u>-ion 'state'</u>

'the absence of action'

Unit 4

4.1
a. to make familiar
b. to make tough
c. to make pure
d. to become active
e. to make soft

4.2
a. unionize
b. solidify
c. intensify
d. motivate
e. alienate
f. decorate
g. beautify
h. redden
i. Italianize
j. italicize

4.3
a. The setting sun <u>reddens</u> the sky.
b. Don't <u>Americanize</u> your culture too much.
c. The army <u>terrorized</u> the citizens.
d. Tina Turner's wonderful singing <u>captivated</u> the audience.
e. Spices <u>intensify</u> the flavor of food.
f. John's face <u>reddened</u> with embarrassment.
g. English students must learn to <u>hyphenate</u> correctly.
h. A lot of money has been spent to <u>deepen</u> the Panama Canal.

Answer Key

i.   Teenagers often <u>idolize</u> pop stars.
j.   Big dogs will tend to <u>frighten</u> small children.

4.4
a.   The <u>tender</u> steak tasted good.
     The steak was <u>tenderized</u> in the mustard marinade.
b.   The sun <u>brightens</u> this area of the garden in the late afternoon.
     The <u>bright</u> sun hurt my eyes.
c.   The <u>final</u> exam was given on the last day of class.
     The businessmen will <u>finalize</u> the deal on Friday.
d.   Please <u>validate</u> your ticket with the parkade supervisor.
     You need a <u>valid</u> ticket to park here.
e.   We visited my sister-in-law in the <u>hospital</u>.
     She was <u>hospitalized</u> on Monday.
f.   Society <u>institutionalizes</u> violent criminals.
     Prisons are one type of <u>institution</u>.

4.5
a.   motivation   motive
b.   intensification intense
c.   decoration   decor
d.   civilization   civil
e.   purification   pure
f.   liberalization   liberal

4.6
a.   complication
b.   salivate
c.   regulation
d.   calculation
e.   mediate
f.   rotate
g.   meditation
h.   locate
i.   investigation
f.   populate

4.7
a.   The Romans <u>civilized</u> the Germans.
     But the Roman <u>civilization</u> was eventually destroyed by German tribes.
b.   Some students lack <u>motivation</u>.

Answer Key

The pursuit of a high grade <u>motivates</u> most students.

c.   <u>Familiarize</u> yourself with the text.

       <u>Familiarization</u> with the text will help you pass the final examination.

d.   The city of Vancouver <u>purifies</u> its drinking water.

       Water <u>purification</u> is important in maintaining good health.

e.   The <u>idolization</u> of movie stars is widespread among teenagers.

       My wife has <u>idolized</u> Elvis since his death.

Post-test

Part A

a.   'to become or make a Canadian'

b.   'to make public'

c.   'to make light'

d.   'to become a captivate'

e.   'to make diverse'

Part B

a.   Fertile fields produce lots of crops. Farmers must therefore <u>fertilize</u> their fields.

b.   On Halloween the children got a big fright. Dressed as a ghost, Sarah <u>frightened</u> them to tears. Sarah's mother <u>penalized</u> her by making her stay inside for the rest of the night.

c.   Buttons will <u>activate</u> an elevator. An active elevator goes up and down; however, sudden stops and starts will <u>roughen</u> the ride for passengers.

Part C

a.   You can <u>thicken</u> a sauce by adding cornstarch.

       My grandfather spoke with a <u>thick</u> Irish accent.

       The sauce's <u>thickness</u> was just right.

b.   Engineers measured the <u>deepness</u> of the lake.

       His voice <u>deepened</u> when he reached fifteen.

       This lake is <u>deep</u>.

c.   Doctors use <u>sterile</u> needles for injections.

       The <u>sterilization</u> of needles is necessary.

       Surgeons <u>sterilize</u> their hands before surgery.

Unit 5

5.1
a. Turkish
b. Danish
c. Finnish
d. Scottish
e. Polish
f. Spanish
g. British
h. English
i. Irish

5.2
a. <u>Kenyan</u> coffee is exported to many places in the world.
b. I know a <u>Cantonese</u> couple.
c. The Americans bombed the <u>Vietnamese</u> countryside during the war.
d. Jack became lost in the <u>Scottish mountains</u>.
e. I don't know <u>the Burmese language</u>.
f. These fossils are <u>Moroccan</u>.
g. <u>The Egyptian pyramids</u> have fascinated people for centuries.
h. He was <u>Malaysian</u> and she was <u>African</u>.

5.3
a. 'without blame'
b. 'resembling life'
c. 'every year'
d. 'resembling a coward'
e. 'without fear'
f. 'one that wars'

5.4
a. sixth
b. birdlike
c. childless
d. weekly
e. fatherly
f. lasting
g. homeless
h. noiseless

5.5

a. Poverty in the U.S. will <u>endure</u> for many more years.
    Poverty is an <u>enduring</u> problem in the U.S.
b. We saw a <u>countless</u> number of birds on the beach.
    We couldn't <u>count</u> the number of birds on the beach.
c. The Eskimo dog of the Canadian North is <u>wolflike</u>.
    The hikers saw a <u>wolf</u> in the forest.
d. Jackie gets paid once a <u>month</u>.
    Her <u>monthly</u> paycheck is spent on rent, bills and food.
e. Bob has <u>seven</u> cars.
    He bought his <u>seventh</u> car last year.
f. A <u>friendless</u> person has no <u>friends</u>.

5.6

a. Many people still think that O. J. Simpson is <u>guiltless</u> in the murder of his wife.
b. The children saw a <u>ghostly</u> (or ghostlike) image in the graveyard.
c. <u>Healing plants</u> are used throughout the world.
d. Jack was in the <u>twentieth position</u> in the long lineup for tickets.
e. These plants have <u>bell-like flowers</u>.

5.7

a. 'tending to agree'
b. 'tending to sleep'
c. 'full of glory'
d. 'characterized by education' or 'having education'
e. 'like a child'
f. 'somewhat brown'
g. 'of, relating to nature'
h. 'of, relating to quality'
i. 'tending to abuse'
j. 'full of pity'
k. 'filling a cup'
i. 'of, relating to Satan' or 'like Satan'
m. 'of, relating to geometry'
n. 'of, relating to a molecule'

5.8

a. mouthful
b. blackish
c. assertive

d.   medicinal
e.   itchy
f.   workable
g.   babyish
h.   fiftyish

5.9
a.   Copper is a <u>metal</u>.
      This chair is <u>metallic</u>.
b.   The politician is full of <u>hope</u> about the next election.
      She is <u>hopeful</u> that she will win.
c.   Susan's <u>girlish</u> smile charms everyone.
      Susan has two children: a <u>girl</u> and a boy.
d.   Jack sweeps the <u>dirt</u> under the carpet.
      He also leaves the <u>dirty</u> dishes in the sink.
e.   The <u>faded</u> newspapers lay in the street.
      Newspapers will <u>fade</u> if they are in the sun.
f.   Businesses like to <u>employ</u> trained people.
      Trained people are <u>employable</u>.
g.   Picking apples is <u>seasonal</u> work.
      Autumn is a colorful <u>season</u>.
h.   My wife <u>selected</u> some paint for the house.
      You have to be a <u>selective</u> consumer in today's society.

5.10
a.   Mary is <u>thirtyish</u>.
b.   His <u>ragged</u> clothes appalled everyone.
c.   Pigs aren't <u>furry</u>.
d.   His <u>spacious</u> holds lots of people.
e.   My uncle is <u>oldish</u>.
f.   Byron is a <u>mysterious poet</u>.
g.   We want a <u>reliable worker</u>.

Post-test

Part A
a.   night + ly 'every night'
b.   exhaust + ive 'tending to exhaust'
c.   fiction + al 'of or relating to fiction'
d.   Nepal + ese 'from Nepal, of or relating to Nepal'
e.   bigot + ed 'like a bigot'

Answer Key   163

Part B

a.   She shows much <u>grace</u> when she dances.
       After years of practice, ballerinas are <u>graceful</u> dancers.
       Someone without grace is <u>graceless</u>.
b.   The Robinson family spent a <u>restful</u> Sunday afternoon watching videos.
       Children need their <u>rest</u>.
       My brother spent a <u>restless</u> night in the hospital because it was so noisy.
c.   Bob was <u>realistic</u> about his job opportunities.
       Sarah has a ring with <u>real</u> diamonds.
       Bob is a <u>realist</u> about his job opportunities.

Part C

a.   uneasy
b.   quiet
c.   uncertain
d.   unafraid
e.   happy
f.   crying
g.   easy
h.   expectant

Unit 6

6.1

a.   oculist
b.   sponsor
c.   donee
d.   florist
e.   evacuee
f.   mentor
g.   hedonist
h.   traitor

6.2

a.   'one that specializes in languages'
b.   'one that receives a lease'
c.   'one that gives'
d.   'one that deceives'
e.   'thing that applies'
f.   'one that examines'

Answer Key

g.   'one that specializes in science'

6.3
a.   thank
b.   love
c.   save
d.   one
e.   honor, pride
f.   many
g.   superior position
h.   purify in water

6.4
a.   When the ship sank, all the sailors were <u>saved</u>.
        The <u>salvage</u> washed upon the shore.
b.   The child showed <u>gratitude</u> for the many birthday gifts.
        The child will <u>thank</u> everyone who brought a gift.
c.   It's nice to be <u>free from</u>.
        Tony spends his <u>leisure</u> playing golf.
d.   The farmer uses his <u>tractor</u> to plough his corn field.
        His truck is sometimes used to <u>pull</u> wagons full of hay.
e.   The <u>brave</u> firefighter pulled the child out of the burning house.
        The firefighter was given a medal for his <u>courage</u>.
f.   A <u>strong</u> person can stay in the forest over night without being afraid.
        Sally showed a lot of <u>fortitude</u> by staying in the forest alone for the whole night.
g.   The politician was noted for his moral <u>rectitude</u>.
        Sometimes it's hard to find an <u>honest</u> politician.
h.   The teacher gave the student <u>latitude</u> to do whatever he wanted.
        The student was <u>free</u> to do whatever he wanted.
i.   The spy was given an impossible <u>mission</u>.
        The agency <u>sent</u> the spy to Lagos.

6.5
a.   amplify
b.   terrify
c.   educate
d.   testify
e.   enumerate
f.   calculate

6.6

a.	turn aside
b.	rot
c.	sacred
d.	whole
e.	true
f.	end
g.	liquid
h.	gift
i.	strong
j.	right

6.7

a.	Mr. Watson expressed <u>gratitude</u> to those who attended his wife's funeral.
	It will <u>gratify</u> Mr. Watson that so many people attended his wife's funeral.
b.	Do not <u>dignify</u> that silly question with an answer.
	A Prime Minister must show <u>dignity</u> when in office.
c.	Who will <u>baptize</u> the baby?
	The <u>baptism</u> of the baby will take place next Sunday.
d.	Climbers of Mount Everest must have great <u>fortitude</u>.
	The good lunch will <u>fortify</u> them for the hike.
e.	They will <u>rectify</u> the spelling mistakes before handing the assignment in to the teacher.
	Priests and ministers must show <u>rectitude</u> at all times.
f.	Canada is a <u>union</u> of provinces and territories.
	During the last election the issue of unemployment <u>unified</u> the various parties.
g.	Ghosts and goblins <u>horrify</u> children.
	The <u>horror</u> of seeing the thief made the children scream.

6.8

a.	affirm
b.	shorten
c.	enlarge
d.	stray
e.	give completely
f.	rot
g.	list
h.	frighten

Post-test

Part A
a.　tail + or　　　'sew (clothes)'
b.　arbit + er　　'decide (a dispute)'
c.　pac + ify　　　'calm'
d.　nomin + ate　'name'
e.　ampl + ify　　'great, strong'
f.　horr + or　　　'frighten'
g.　celebr +ate　'merry'
h.　relig + ion　　'worship'
i.　simil + itude　'similar'
j.　outr + age　　'insult, offend'

Part B
a.　dedicate
b.　arbitrate
c.　terminate
d.　baptize

Part C
a.　termination
b.　creation
c.　unity
d.　similitude

Unit 7

7.1
a.　hilarious
b.　tragic
c.　rigid
d.　sociable
e.　solar
f.　juvenile
g.　feminine
h.　natal

7.2
a.　'of or relating to rot'
b.　'capable of reproduction'

Answer Key

c. 'of or relating to flowers'
d. 'capable of change'
e. 'of or relating to severity'
f. 'like a cat or having the nature of a cat'
g. 'of or relating to warmth'
h. 'full of good taste'
I. 'of or relating to a mother'
j. 'of or relating to a male'

7.3

a.	credible	believable
b.	divine	godly
c.	frigid	cold
d.	tedious	boring
e.	horrible	fearful
f.	fragile	breakable
g.	noxious	harmful
h.	eternal	everlasting
i.	marine	sea
j.	fluid	flowing

7.4

a. the deep blue <u>sea</u>
a <u>marine</u> climate
The Mediterranean <u>sea</u> is full of <u>marine</u> life.

b. the hot <u>sun</u>
a <u>solar</u> eclipse
<u>Solar</u> panels store heat from the <u>sun</u>.

c. a <u>mortal</u> injury
a slow <u>death</u>
A <u>mortal</u> illness will cause <u>death</u>.

d. a bright full <u>moon</u>
a <u>lunar</u> crater
In a <u>lunar</u> eclipse the earth comes between the sun and the <u>moon</u>.

e. a <u>floral</u> decoration
the smell of a <u>flower</u>
A <u>floral</u> pattern is made up of <u>flowers</u>.

f. the <u>manual</u> worker
dirty <u>hands</u>
<u>Manual</u> labor means to labor with the <u>hands</u>.

7.5

a. The exam seemed to last for an <u>eternity</u>.
    Some people desire <u>eternal</u> life.
b. Some hockey players are very <u>superstitious</u>.
    Some people claim there is a connection between religion and <u>superstition</u>.
c. <u>Rigidity</u> is the state of being stiff.
    When I was a child, my mother had <u>rigid</u> rules about doing homework.
d. They threw the <u>putrid</u> meat into the garbage.
    Meat will <u>putrefy</u> if left in the hot sun.
e. The brothers are <u>similar</u> in appearance.
    The <u>similarity</u> of the twins is striking.
f. Some <u>religious</u> people worship every day.
    Islam is a major <u>religion</u>.
g. The company is going to <u>terminate</u> Mary's job.
    Sue has a <u>terminal</u> disease.
h. It is an <u>outrage</u> that politicians do not keep their election promises.
    The teenager's <u>outrageous</u> behavior shocked everyone.
i. Frank was <u>oblivious</u> to the noise the children made in the backyard.
    Some people seek <u>oblivion</u> through drugs and alcohol.
j. The comic's jokes caused great <u>hilarity</u>.
    The <u>hilarious</u> comic made everyone laugh.

Post-test

Part A
a. missile
b. serious
c. oral
d. horrible
e. molar
f. caustic
g. feline

Part B
a. The politician only had <u>nominal</u> success, and soon became unpopular.
    The political <u>nominee</u> thanked all his supporters.
    Will you <u>nominate</u> me for the committee?
b. The <u>horrid</u> accident left two people dead.
    The <u>horror</u> of the fire gave the children nightmares.
    Nightmares about the fire <u>horrify</u> the children.
c. He made a <u>terrible</u> mistake when he left the keys in the car.

Answer Key

Terrorists use <u>terror</u> to intimidate civilians.
Big dogs <u>terrify</u> small children.

Unit 8

8.1
a.   readability
b.   responsibility
c.   portable
d.   feasibility
e.   reliable
f.   credible
g.   sociability
h.   transferability
i.   defensibility
j.   accessible
k.   manageable

8.2
a.   The <u>readability</u> of this book made it a best seller.
     People say that this book is very <u>readable</u>.
b.   Because Jacob had been in prison, people doubted his <u>credibility</u>.
     The police thought that his story was not <u>credible</u>.
c.   May is a <u>reliable</u> worker.
     People traveling to work on the train depend on the <u>reliability</u> of the
system.
d.   You are <u>responsible</u> for your books.
     It is your <u>responsibility</u> to look after your books.
e.   <u>Visibility</u> was terrible because of the thick fog.
     The shore was barely <u>visible</u> through the thick fog.

8.3
a.   dominant
b.   obedient
c.   competence
d.   resistance
e.   opulent
f.   tolerance
g.   presence
h.   important
i.   absence
j.   brilliance

8.4

a. The twins were <u>absent</u> from school today.
   Their <u>absence</u> was due to the flu.
b. Your dog's <u>obedience</u> is admirable.
   Your dog is very <u>obedient</u>.
c. We want to try a <u>different</u> approach to this problem.
   One <u>difference</u> between you and me is that I enjoy classical music and you don't.
d. What an <u>elegant</u> room this is!
   I like the <u>elegance</u> of this room.
e. The <u>persistence</u> of the economic downturn in Asia bothered people worldwide.
   Raymond had a <u>persistent</u> headache that lasted for three days.

8.5

a. angular
b. single
c. spectacle
d. titular
e. testicular
f. triangle

8.6

a. 'a system of <u>muscles</u>'
b. 'the whole number of <u>people</u> in a country or region'
c. 'shaped like a <u>rectangle</u>'
d. 'to divide into <u>triangles</u>'
e. 'inhabited by many <u>people</u>'
f. 'having the quality or form of a <u>circle</u>'
g. 'the <u>people</u> in general'

8.7

a. inscription
b. transcription
c. deception
d. subscription
e. reception
a. reduction
g. absorption
h. implication

Answer Key   171

i. junction
j. conception
k. destruction
a. seduction

8.8
a. destructive
b. prescriptive
c. deceptive
d. absorptive
e. productive
f. perceptive
g. receptive
f. seductive

8.9
a. subversion
b. delusion
c. provision
e. suspension
f. inclusion
g. diversion
h. erosion
i. conversion

8.10
a. admission
b. procession
c. recession
d. commission
e. transmission
f. emission

8.11
a. invasive
b. explosive
c. recessive
d. decisive
e. inclusive
f. subversive
g. evasive

Answer Key

h.   permissive

Post-test

Part A
a.   He never took into account the <u>workability</u> of the project.
       John's solution to the problem is <u>workable</u>.
b.   The <u>brilliant</u> diamond glistened in the sunlight.
       The <u>brilliance</u> of the sun blinded him.
c.   A <u>triangular</u> figure has three sides.
       A <u>triangle</u> has three sides.
d.   Paula's <u>conception</u> of the project was different from Bob's.
       Can you <u>conceive</u> of a different way to make money?
e.   Alcoholism is a <u>divisive</u> problem within society.
       Alcoholism can <u>divide</u> a family.
       The family <u>division</u> can sometimes be permanent.
f.   I got my parents' <u>permission</u> to go to the movies.
       My parents <u>permit</u> me to go to the movies.
       <u>Permissive</u> parents give their children too much freedom.

Part B
a.   joined
b.   applied
c.   destroyed
d.   applying
e.   exceeding
f.   defended

Part C
a.   verb
b.   noun
c.   adjective
d.   verb
e.   noun
f.   adjective
g.   noun
h.   noun
i.   adjective
j.   adjective
k.   adjective
l.   noun

Answer Key

Unit 9

9.1
a.   limits
b.   flowers
c.   say or speak
d.   believe
e.   hearing
f.   taken or held

9.2
a.   annuity
b.   fluctuate
c.   docile
d.   fragment
e.   corpse
f.   fraternity

9.3
a.   true
b.   false
c.   false
d.   true
e.   true
f.   false

9.4
a.   small flower
b.   mathematical fragment
c.   listeners
d.   length of time
e.   flowing
f.   body of material
g.   foreigner
h.   a saying

9.5
a.   law
b.   read and write
c.   great

d.	middle
e.	small
f.	movement or motion

9.6
a.	genesis
b.	legible
c.	migrant
d.	maternity
e.	locate
f.	gratitude

9.7
a.	true
b.	true
c.	false
d.	false
e.	true
f.	true

9.8
a.	rocket
b.	dying
c.	tip
d.	undertaker
e.	freedom
f.	purpose
g.	not worldwide
h.	dignified woman

9.9
a.	people
b.	numbers
c.	feeling
d.	wrong
e.	worked
f.	birth

9.10
a.	navigate
b.	pendulous

Answer Key

c.   plenary
d.   paternity
e.   rotary
f.   punctuate

9.11
a.   true
b.   false
c.   false
d.   true
e.   true
f.   false

9.12
a.   people
b.   count
c.   punish
d.   circular building
e.   hanging
f.   power
g.   inactive
h.   straight intestine

9.13
a.   senses
b.   skill or ability
c.   empty
d.   resemble
e.   true
f.   holy

9.14
a.   visual
b.   vivid
c.   terrain
d.   valor
e.   various
f.   terminus

9.15
a.   true

Answer Key

b. true
c. false
d. true
e. false
f. true

9.16
a. resemblance
b. aware
c. difference
d. instruction
e. lively
f. go to see
g. worth
h. empty

Post-test

Part A

a.	valiant	✓	'courageous'
			'fearful'
b.	testate		'having an invalid will'
		✓	'having a valid will'
c.	alienate	✓	'to become hostile to others'
			'to become friendly with others'
d.	fraternize		'to be unfriendly'
		✓	'to be friendly'
e.	literal	✓	'relating to the exact letter'
			'imaginative'
f.	primitive		'cultured'
		✓	'from the earliest times'
g.	pacifism	✓	'opposition to war'
			'support of war'
h.	penalty	✓	'punishment'
			'reward'
i.	navigable		'that ships cannot travel on'
		✓	'that ships can travel on'
j.	sensuous		' of or relating to the mind'
		✓	' of or relating to the senses'

Part B

Answer Key

177

a. The actor was told that he got the leading role in the play right after his <u>audition</u>.

His voice was barely <u>audible</u> because there was so much noise coming from the street.

b. The prime minister said he would <u>liberate</u> all the political prisoners currently in jail.

A democratic government must protect the <u>liberty</u> of its citizens.

c. The <u>naval</u> commander met with the press after the accident aboard the ship.

Canada has a small <u>navy</u>.

d. The railway <u>terminates</u> in Prince George.

Its <u>terminus</u> is in Prince George.

e. The Rolling Stones are still one of the most <u>popular</u> rock bands in the world.

Most of the people who <u>populate</u> this area are from the province of Quebec.

Unit 10

10.1
a. in
b. back
c. together
d. down
e. again
f. forward
g. back
h. to
i. to
a. beforehand

10.2
a. reflect
   deflect
b. deject
   reject
   project
c. immigrate
   emigrate
d. permit
   transmit

Answer Key

emit

remit

i.   induct

abduct

conduct

deduct

10.3

a.   true

b.   false

c.   true

d.   true

e.   false

f.   false

10.4

1

a.   preceded

b.   recede

2

a.   attracts

b.   protract

c.   detracts

3

a.   collapsed

b.   elapsed

c.   relapsed

10.5

a.   out

b.   out

c.   out

d.   to

e.   on

f.   into

g.   thoroughly

h.   forth

10.6

a. erupt
   disrupt
   corrupt
b. propel
   dispel
   expel
   repel
c. revert
   avert
   divert
d. diverge
   converge
e. import
   export
f. repress
   depress
   compress

10.7
a. false
b. true
c. true
d. false
e. true
f. false

10.8
1a. compulsion
b. expulsion
c. propulsion

2a. digress
b. regressed
c. progress
d. ingress

3a. destruction
b. construction
c. instructions

Answer Key

4a. invoked
b. revoked
c. evokes
d. advocate

Post-test

Part A
a. project
b. describe
c. inhale
d. proceed
e. succeed
f. revoke
g. invert
h. perceive
i. converge
j. detract

Part B
a. be away
b. look into
c. climb up
d. drive out
e. send away
f. carry to another place
g. burst out
h. put money in
i. cut apart

Unit 11

11.1
a. seabird
b. doorbell
c. fisheagle
d. horseshoe
e. housetop
f. paperwork
g. bookwork
h. workbook

Answer Key

11.2

a. doorknob
b. boyfriend
c. workbench
d. papermaker
e. dogsled
f. doghouse
g. doorman
h. seashore
i. lakeshore
j. riverbank

11.3

a. doorkeeper
b. housewife
c. hothead
d. seahorse
e. wolffish
f. wolfhound
g. dogfight
h. in the doghouse

11.4

a. herbicide
b. patricide
c. suicide
d. homicide
e. spermicide
f. insecticide
g. genocide

11.5

a. phraseology
b. anthropology
c. theology
d. graphology
e. zoology
f. pathology
g. radiology
h. astrology

Answer Key

11.6
a.   agoraphobia
b.   homophobia
c.   xenophobia
d.   arachnophobia
e.   claustrophobia

11.7
a.   hydrometer
b.   bibliophile
c.   telephone
d.   ecology
e.   photograph
f.   telescope
g.   thermometer
h.   psychology
i.   monarchy
j.   unicycle

11.8
a.   principal or chief
b.   traveler
c.   management
d.   art or science
e.   one
f.   sound
g.   speaks
h.   unnatural attraction
i.   tendency
j.   study

Post-test

Part A
a.   phonograph
b.   stethoscope
c.   unisex
d.   chronometer
e.   psychosomatic

Part B

a.   boathouse

b.   houseboat

Part C

a.

A Canadian judge will begin a crash course in <u>musicology</u> on Monday when he begins hearing evidence in a court case. A man claims he co-wrote several songs with a famous singer and <u>songwriter</u>, but was not given any credits for them.

b.

An <u>iceberg</u> is a large mass of ice in the sea that has originated on land. Many result from the breaking off of ice from glaciers. In the north <u>icebergs</u> originate chiefly from <u>Greenland</u>; in the south most break off from Antarctica, an icy land mass covering 14,300,000 square <u>kilometers</u>.

c.

North American birds live in a variety of habitats. <u>Seagulls</u> and <u>sandpipers</u> live close to water. <u>Meadowlarks</u> like fields and meadows, whereas <u>blackbirds</u> like marshes and fields. Jays and robins prefer forests.

Glossary

Prefixes

ab-, a-	'away, from, off'
ad-, at-, as-, ap-, af-, ac-, ag-, ar-, al-, an-, ab-, a-	'to, toward'
anti-	'opposed to, against'
co-	'fellow, together'
com-, con-, col-, cor-, co-	'with, together, completely'
de-	'remove, remove from'
dis-, di-	'not, do the opposite of, apart, away, aside'
en-, em-	'to make, cause to be, put into or onto'
ex-, e-	'former,'out, from, thoroughly'
fore-	'before, beforehand'
in-, il-, im-, ir-	'not'
in-, il-, im-, ir-	'in, into, on, upon, very"
mis-	'bad(ly), wrong(ly)'
non-	'not'
per-	'through, thoroughly'
pre-	'in advance, before'
pro-	'favor, favoring, forward, forth, out'
re-	'again, back'
semi-	'half, partly, partial'
sub-	'below, under, secondary'
super-	'superior, exceeding'
trans-, tran-	'across, over, beyond'
un-	'not, do the opposite of'

Suffixes

-able, -ible	'capable of, fit for, tending to'
-age	'act, process, result, state'
-al, -ar	'of, relating to'
-an, -ian	'a native of, a supporter, believer, one that works with, of relating to, from'
-ance	'act, state'
-ate	'make, cause to become, become'

-ation	'act, process'
-ative	'of, relating to, tending to'
-dom	'office, realm, status, state'
-ed	'having, characterized by, like'
-ee	'person that is, receives, or does'
-en	'make, cause'
-er	'one or thing that does, one that makes, works, a native of, one that is'
-ery, -ry	'state, condition, activity, a place for'
-ese	'a native of, of, relating to, from'
-ful	'full of, tending to, like, filling'
-hood	'period (time), state, quality, shared state'
-ic	'of, relating to, like'
-ical	'of, relating to, like'
-id	'of, relating to'
-ie, -y	'a dear little one, one that is'
-ify, -fy	'make, make similar to, become'
-ile	'capable of, characteristic of'
-ine	'of, like, having the nature of'
-ing	'act, process, result, that does'
-ion	'act, state, result'
-ish	'of, relating to, like, tending to, about, somewhat'
-ism	'doctrine, act, state'
-ist	'one that does, one that plays, makes, one that specializes in, one that advocates'
-ite	'a native of'
-itude	'act, state, quality'
-ity, -ty	'state, quality, degree'
-ive	'tending to, making'
-ize	'make, put into, become, make, engage in'
-less	'without'
-like	'like, resembling'
-ly	'like, resembling, every'
-ment	'act, state'
-ness	'state, condition'
-or	'one or thing that does'
-ous, -ious	'having, possessing, full of'
-ship	'office, skill, state, condition'
-ster	'one that makes, one that participates, one that is'
-th	'state, condition', used for numbers in order
-ure	'act, state, result'

Glossary

-y	'full of, like, tending to'

Some Common Roots

ali, altr	'other, different'
ann, enn	'year'
aud	'hear'
cap, capt	'take, hold'
capit, capt	'head, chief, leader'
cert	'sure, true'
corp	'body'
cred	'believe'
dict	'say, speak'
doc, doct	'teach'
dur	'hard, strong, lasting'
fac, fact	'do, make'
fin	'end, complete, limit'
flor	'flower'
flu, fluct	'flow'
frag, fract	'break'
frater, fratr	'brother'
gen	'birth, produce, race'
grat	'pleasing, thankful'
jur, just	'law'
leg	'law, read'
liber	'free'
lit	'letter, read, word'
loc	'location, place'
magn	'great'
mater, matr	'mother'
medi	'middle'
migr	'move to new place'
min	'least, smallest'
mit, miss	'send'
mor, mort	'death'
mot	'move'
nat	'born, birth'
nav	'boat, ship'
numer	'number'
oper, opus	'work'
pac	'peace'

Glossary

pat, pass	'suffer, experience, feel'
pater, patr	'father'
pen	'penalty, wrong'
pend	'hang, heavy'
plen	'full'
popul	'people'
pot	'power, ability'
prim	'first'
punct	'point, prick, pierce'
reg, rect	'rule, right, straight'
rot	'round, turn'
sanct	'holy'
sent, sens	'feel, aware'
simil, simul	'similar, resemble'
techn	'skill, ability'
term	'end, boundary, limit'
terr	'earth, land'
test	'witness'
tut, tuit	'teach'
vac	'empty'
val	'value, worth, brave'
var	'change, different'
ver	'true, truth'
vis	'see'
vit, viv	'life, alive, lively'

Common Roots in Compounds

arch-	'chief, principal'
-arch	'ruler'
-archy	'rule, government'
astro-	'star, outer space'
-cide	'kill'
geo-	'earth, ground'
-graph	'draw, write, picture, record'
-graphy	'science, writing, describing'
hydro-	'water, hydrogen'
-logy	'study, doctrine, science, discussion'
matri-	'mother'
-meter	'measure'

Glossary

-naut	'sailor, traveler'
-nomy	'arrangement, science, management'
-path	'person suffering, medical practitioner'
patri-	'father'
-phile	'lover, loving'
-philia	'tendency, unnatural attraction'
-phobia	'fear, hatred'
-phone	'sound, speak'
psycho-	'mind'
-scope	'see, observe'
uni-	'one'